“I have been teaching and preachi[illegible] discovered this jewel, an in-depth study of Korah’s rebellion. It is a guide to mining any scriptural passage, for beginners or seasoned pastors like me. Lisa’s simple Bible study methods unearth fascinating details in the Old Testament. The chapters are short and include simple exegetical practices and questions for personal application. It is extremely useful and interesting for personal or group study or to help you teach the Bible with greater personal application, accuracy, and completeness. I will buy it for gifts and for myself.”

—**Barbara Yandell,** President, Hope for the Nations

“Lisa Lewis Koster is one of the best Bible researchers I know. It’s amazing how she can pull information together from biblical times and make it understandable for her audience.”

—**Kathy Bruins**, author and founder of The Well Ministry for Creatives

“In this book Lisa unlocks priceless treasures from a remote Old Testament story. It will give you a much deeper appreciation for the wisdom, love, and power of God, and lead you to worship him in authentic, new ways. You will get practical new insights into yourself as Lisa reveals how the fallen nature we’ve inherited from Adam opposes God. Lisa guides readers along the path of humility, conviction, repentance, and the life changes needed to live with joyful contentment. Only authors who’ve walked through dark valleys are able to take us to the mountains like this.”

—**John Sawyer**, Torah Club Bible Study Leader, former CEO of Clear Bible, Inc.

“How can we live with contentment? Author and Bible teacher Lisa Lewis Koster explores Korah’s rebellion while offering a strong overview of its historical context. She personalizes ancient practices to close the gap of centuries. *Enough coaches us to fuller biblical literacy—and life.*”

—**Cynthia Beach**, author of *The Surface of Water* and *Creative Juices for Writers*

"Lisa seems to effortlessly integrate biblical history, stories, and truths, as well as personal challenges for the reader, in this easy-to-read study of Korah's Rebellion in Numbers 16."

—**James L. Koetje**, former state representative, Michigan

Do you compare? Do you complain? Glean from Koster's wealth of research as you study the Bible using her book, *Enough.* Lisa simplifies her teaching with study tools such as graphs, charts, illustrations, questions, and impactful blurbs to reinforce her teaching of Biblical truths. This rich study will leave you longing for her next one!

—**Darlene Larson**, author and speaker,
Grief-loss & Life Purpose Coach® at Hearts with a Purpose

"Lisa's excellent book will help those not familiar with the Bible and those like me who've spent a lifetime in the Word. Lisa helps us face our jealousy and rebellion against God, while humbly sharing her own struggles. I highly recommend this book for a group Bible study."

—**Tom Hooker**, former state representative, Michigan

"This Bible study will intrigue you. *Enough* is the result of insightful research by Lisa Lewis Koster into often overlooked specifics. This study brings us deeper into the Old Testament and then bridges into the New Testament. Questions at the end of each chapter help to apply what's been learned. An excellent, thoughtfully written study."

—**Beverly J. Porter**, author of *One Amazing Night: A Christmas Story*

Enough

Enough

Finding Contentment in a World of Wanting and Wandering

Lisa Lewis Koster

Enough

Published in the United States of America by Credo House Publishers,
a division of Credo Communications LLC, Grand Rapids, Michigan
credohousepublishers.com

ISBN: 978-1-62586-263-1

Cover and interior design by Frank Gutbrod
Editing by Vanessa Carroll

Printed in the United States of America
First Edition

Contents

Introduction

As soon as I heard the crunching of tires rolling up the gravel driveway, I ran and hid behind the sofa. This had already been a rough year for me. My mom began working full-time outside our home, and my fourth-grade self did not like it. Not one bit! My dad was returning after attending parent-teacher conferences for the first time, and I just did not see this working out well for me.

I was right.

My dad relayed his conversation with my teacher to my mom. "And I told her, 'Don't you *ever* give her an A unless that paper is perfect!'" I would think most parents would be happy if their child came home with an A, even if they did get a question or two wrong. But my dad's words merely confirmed what I already knew. I needed to be perfect.

When I started the ninth grade, my dad told me, "You *will* graduate at the top of your class." That thought had never even occurred to me. But I did what was expected. I didn't deceive myself into thinking I was smarter than everyone else. I just followed the rules and put in the work (not to mention a lot of extra-credit). Honestly, I did not want to have to hear about it if I didn't land that top spot.

I came away from church believing the same lie. It was my understanding that God was keeping track of everything I did wrong, and I had better make sure that the good outweighed the bad. The message seemed consistent with the one I heard at home.

Be perfect.

I grew up in a church without Bibles in the pews. I heard Scripture in the services, but never in context. I knew reading the Bible was a good thing to do. The problem was, I never made it out of Genesis. And after multiple attempts, I gave up.

I met my husband Bob, then Jesus. In that order. I learned that the Bible is not just one book but a compilation of sixty-six books. And I could start reading any one of them. Who knew? I was almost thirty-years-old before I began reading the Bible, but once I got started, I was hooked! Although at first I was confused. And surprised.

Before I read the Bible for myself, I thought Bible people were perfect, but many of the people I read about were pretty messed up. Even the ones who seemed to have it all together had their shortcomings, just like me. I think that's why some say the Bible is like a mirror. If we look at enough people, we're bound to see someone just like ourselves.

This book will focus on a messed up man named Korah, who was anything but content. Through his story, we will learn why God despises our grumbling. We will also identify and work to eliminate our own discontent, making room in our lives for the contentment God desires for us.

As we study Korah's rebellion, we will take the time to look at the historical context of people and events to give us a better understanding of God's Word and His message to us today. By choosing to spend more time with God we reap the benefit of lessening the impact of the world's influence on us.

Each short chapter ends with a few questions to help you dig deeper into Scripture. There are also some self-discovery questions to help pinpoint where your thinking may be off-track in your quest to be more like Jesus. Finally, throughout the book I also introduce some of the tools I used as I pulled this study together. My goal is not just to explain what I think is a really cool Bible story; I also want to equip you to better understand any part of Scripture.

This book serves as an Israelites 101 class of sorts. Much of what we learn will help to explain other parts of the Old Testament. And we really can't fully understand the New Testament without knowing the Old Testament. Especially where Jesus is concerned. His words often point back to the Old Testament, which is one of the reasons why the Jewish leadership felt so threatened by Him.

Why did I write a book about contentment and this obscure character named Korah? I finally realized it is because I *was* Korah. Like him, I only had my eyes on the top spot. Nothing else was acceptable. I kept on striving for perfection so that maybe, finally, I would be good enough. But God has redeemed my perfectionism and turned it into an eye for detail. Without it I could not have written this book.

If you are not familiar with the Bible, then you are in the right place. This book was written for my former self. I know what it is like to be an adult with zero Bible knowledge, so as we look at Scripture, we will take it slow. We will get to know the characters and learn why they do what they do. In fact, as a novice, you may actually have an advantage because you may see details that those more familiar with Scripture tend to gloss over.

If you are well-versed in Scripture, this book is for you as well. The account of Korah's rebellion in Numbers 16 is a strange story—one that does not make a lot of sense until we pull together all the pieces scattered throughout Scripture. You may find many "aha" moments as you work through this study. And, like me, you may also have a few, "Why didn't I ever notice this before?" moments as well.

Reading the Bible is unique. It is the only book you will ever read with the author right there with you every time you pick it up, so it is important to always begin time in God's Word with prayer. God makes many promises to us in His Word, and He loves it when we claim them.

Always begin time in God's Word with prayer.

Before I begin reading and studying the Bible, I pray something like this: "God, I thank You for the gift of Your Word. I pray that Your Holy Spirit will help me to understand what I am reading and to help me remember what You are teaching me. I ask this in Jesus' name, Amen."

In my prayer, I asked God for what He promised to give us in John 14:26. In that chapter, Jesus is explaining to His disciples that He will be going away, but that God will not leave them alone. "The Holy Spirit, whom the Father will send in my name, will *teach* you all things and will *remind* you of everything I have said to you" (NIV emphasis added).

God promises the Holy Spirit will teach us, and part of a teacher's job is to help us understand what we are reading. The purpose of being taught something is to remember it and apply it to our lives. This is also a great way to pray as you memorize Scripture. I pray that God will reveal Himself to you through this book, and that you will find yourself even closer to Him than you were before you started.

PART ONE

The Rebellion

(Numbers 16:1–3)

Chapter 1

The Beginning

A friend once asked me what part of the Bible I was reading. When I replied that I was studying the book of Numbers, her response was, "Bless your heart! People actually read that?" (I would have thought, with her being a CPA, she would be interested in Numbers). Now I will admit the title does not seem too captivating, but we can blame that on the Greeks. They titled the book Numbers because there is a census recorded both at the beginning and toward the end of the book.

The first chapter of Numbers begins with a census of the Israelite men, ages twenty and up, who followed Moses out of slavery in Egypt. The census in chapter twenty-six lists the men of fighting age entering the Promised Land. In between are an action-packed forty years! In my opinion, it is the Hebrew title that more accurately portrays what the book contains. Translated into English, the book was called "In the Desert" or "In the Wilderness."

One scholar says, "Numbers is not a history of Israel, but an essay about the consequences of disobedience."[1] This book will focus on a man named Korah. He was most certainly disobedient, and the consequences he faced were severe. As we work our way through his story, we will identify and learn from his mistakes. In doing this, we can discover the contentment he never found. His story begins in Numbers 16:

> Now Korah the son of Izhar, son of Kohath, son of Levi, and Dathan and Abiram the sons of Eliab, and On the son of Peleth, sons of Reuben, took men. And they rose up before Moses, with a number of the people of Israel, 250 chiefs of the congregation, chosen from the assembly, well-known men. They assembled themselves together against Moses and against Aaron and said to them, "You have gone too far! For all in the congregation are holy, every one of them, and the LORD is among them. Why then do you exalt yourselves above the assembly of the LORD?" (Numbers 16:1–3)

Moses was leading the nation of Israel out of slavery in Egypt and into freedom in the Promised Land. But because of incidents such as this one, what could have been a two-week trip instead lasted forty years.

Korah and all the rebels ended up dying in unique ways. There is also a surprising twist in the story, tucked away in an unlikely place. And here, in the Old Testament, we find sightings of God's grace! But, before we begin looking into the details of Korah's story, first we need to lay a foundation we can build upon. Let's begin by taking a look at the backstory of this group of people.

The book of Numbers begins with God instructing Moses to "take a census of all the congregation of the people of Israel" (Numbers 1:2). This account of Korah's rebellion involves the nation of Israel, but *who* are they? Even if you are familiar with the Israelites, please bear with me. You might be surprised by some of the things we will learn. Some of the most dangerous words we think regarding Scripture are, "I already know all about this." Our goal should be to always read the Bible as if we're seeing the passage for the first time, every time.[2]

Always read the Bible as if we're seeing the passage for the first time.

The story of God's chosen people, the Israelites, begins in Genesis 12:1–3:

> Now the LORD said to Abram, "Go from your country and your kindred and your father's house to the land that I will show you. And I will make of you a great nation, and I will bless you and make your name great, so that you will be a blessing. I will bless those who bless you, and him who dishonors you I will curse, and in you all the families of the earth shall be blessed."

In their old age, Abraham[3] and his wife Sarah were blessed with a child together, a son named Isaac. Isaac had two sons, but it was through Isaac's prolific son Jacob that the number of Abraham's descendants really began to explode. Jacob, his wives, eleven sons and their families eventually moved to Egypt because of a famine. A twelfth son, Joseph, was already there (having been previously sold into slavery by his brothers).[4] There were seventy members of Jacob's family who joined Joseph in Egypt.

Later, "Joseph died, and all his brothers and all that generation. But the people of Israel were fruitful and increased greatly; they multiplied and grew exceedingly strong, so that the land was filled with them" (Exodus 1:6–7). Unfortunately, Joseph and all he did for Egypt was forgotten. That is *why* the new Pharaoh felt threatened by the large number of Israelites in the land and eventually enslaved them. This, however, was no surprise to God.

Look at what God said to Abraham in Genesis 15:13–14: "Know for certain that your offspring will be sojourners in a land that is not theirs and will be servants there, and they will be afflicted for four hundred years. But I will bring judgment on the nation that they serve, and afterward they shall come out with great possessions."

Four hundred years! Not many genealogy buffs are able to trace their family back that far. Even if you could, it's doubtful you would know much about who that person was or what they believed. However, lineage is very important to the Israelite people. They knew the name of their ancestor who traveled into Egypt. The most important question is, did they know the one true God whom their ancestors worshipped?

Digging Deeper

Read Numbers 16:1–35 and record anything that stands out to you or any questions you have about this passage.

List the things in this passage that seem weird to you.

List what you know about this group of people who followed Moses out of Egypt.

Chapter 2

The Travelers

Now that we know a bit about the origin of the Israelites, I have what may seem like a strange question. Have you ever stopped to think about what the suffix *ite* means? According to the Merriam-Webster dictionary,[5] it can mean one of three things. First, it can mean someone who was born in, or is a resident of, a certain area. So this is a good time to ask the question, "*Where* did Korah's rebellion occur?"

At this point in history, God has led the Israelites out of Egypt, but they have not yet reached the Promised Land. They were nomads wandering through the desert, so the first definition of *ite* does not apply. However, the second definition of *ite* refers to a descendant of the person named before the suffix. That begs the question, if the Israelites are the descendants of Jacob, *why* aren't they referred to as Jacobites?

When he was a young man, with his mother's assistance, Jacob tricked his father into giving him a blessing—the blessing that rightfully belonged to his brother Esau. Jacob's mother then insisted that Jacob flee his home and family of origin before Esau could kill him. He traveled to his uncle's home where he became the one tricked. Jacob ended up married to not just one woman, but two. Sisters! After many years of working for his father-in-law Laban, Jacob and his family traveled back to Edom to visit Esau. Jacob sent messengers ahead, while he stayed back with his children and their mothers.

> He took them and sent them across the stream, and everything else that he had. And Jacob was left alone. And a man wrestled with him until the breaking of the day. When the man saw that he did not prevail against Jacob, he touched his hip socket, and Jacob's hip was put out of joint as he wrestled with him. Then he said, "Let me go, for the day has broken." But Jacob said, "I will not let you go unless you bless me." And he said to him, "What is your name?" And he said, "Jacob." Then he said, "Your name shall no longer be called Jacob, but Israel, for you have striven with God and with men, and have prevailed." (Genesis 32:23–28)

God changed Jacob's name to Israel, which means "God strives."[6] That is *why* this group of people are known as the Israelites.

God promised Abraham that his descendants would be more numerous than the stars in the night sky. *How* large had the original Israelite community of seventy become by the time they left Egypt? This is where a census can come in handy! According to the census found in Numbers chapter one, "all those listed of the people of Israel, by their fathers' houses, from twenty years old and upward, every man able to go to war in Israel—all those listed were 603,550" (Numbers 1:45–46).

Scripture does not reveal the exact number of Israelites following Moses. We only know the number of fighting men.

Women and children were not included in that number, nor were the 22,000 Levites who were set apart to serve God at the tabernacle.

But our count of those traveling in the desert with Moses is still not complete. Were you aware there were also individuals not descended from Jacob who were traveling with the Israelites? According to Exodus 12:38, a "mixed multitude also went up with them." Joshua 8:35 confirms there were still foreigners among them as they entered the promised land. This brings us to our third type of *ites*—adherents or followers. Who do you think may have joined the Israelites in their journey out of Egypt?

While we have no way of knowing exactly who joined the Israelites, if I was a slave, I'm pretty sure I would leave with anyone who would take me! Plus, there could be people who came to believe the God of the Israelites was the one true God after experiencing the plagues. In each plague, God was victorious over one of the Egyptian gods. While we cannot be sure of the actual size of this group, some scholars say Moses could have been leading two to three million people![7] Other scholars think these numbers may have been increased by a factor of 10, stating, "In ancient times numbers were used with deliberate exaggeration for rhetorical effect," such as in 1 Samuel 18:7.[8]

I don't know about you, but I have a hard time visualizing a crowd of this size without a point of reference. Because my husband is a University of Michigan football fan, I know that "The Big House" is the largest college football stadium in the United States. It currently has an official capacity of 109,901.[9] Imagine how difficult it would be to try to lead even one stadium full of people. My husband and I were challenged just trying to keep our five children heading in the same direction when we visited an amusement park!

This great nation of Israel was divided into tribes, each headed by one of Jacob's sons. But this is not as straightforward as it may seem. Creating a chart helps to keep track of large amounts of material. Listed on the left side of the following chart are the names of Jacob's sons. On the right side are the names of the twelve tribes of Israel.

Creating a chart helps to keep track of large amounts of material.

JACOB'S SONS (Genesis 35:23–26)	**TRIBES OF ISRAEL** (Numbers 13:1–15)
Reuben	Reuben
Simeon	Simeon
Levi	Judah
Judah	Issachar
Issachar	Ephraim
Zebulun	Benjamin
Joseph	Zebulun
Benjamin	Manasseh
Dan	Dan
Naphtali	Asher
Gad	Naphtali
Asher	Gad

Are you surprised to discover the two lists are not exactly the same? Levi and Joseph were both sons of Jacob, but neither of them is included in the list of the twelve tribes of Israel. Speaking to Joseph soon before his death, Jacob said, "now your two sons, who were born to you in the land of Egypt before I came to you in Egypt, are mine; Ephraim and Manasseh shall be mine, as Reuben and Simeon are" (Genesis 48:5). Now we know where Ephraim and Manasseh came from, but *what* about Levi? We will look at the thirteenth tribe of Levi later in this study.

Digging Deeper

Who do you think may have joined the Israelites in their journey out of Egypt?

God changed Jacob's name to Israel, so why do you think he was still called Jacob after that?

Have you ever led a group of people? If so, describe your experience.

Chapter 3

The Individuals

Moses and Aaron

Now we're going to look more deeply into *who* some of the primary individuals connected to Korah's rebellion are, beginning with Moses. As recorded in Exodus 1-3, Moses was born to Israelite parents enslaved in Egypt at a time when Pharaoh commanded all Israelite boys be killed at birth. When the midwives did not obey Pharaoh's command, he then ordered that every Israelite baby boy be thrown into the Nile River. Moses' ingenious mother managed to hide her son for three months. When that was no longer possible, she laid him in a basket and strategically placed it in the Nile. Moses' mother cleverly obeyed the letter of the law while also ensuring her son's safety. Pharaoh's daughter discovered Moses floating among the reeds, and after he was weaned, she reared him as her son.

For much of the first forty years of his life, Moses was raised and educated as an Egyptian. However, having spent his first, formative years being nursed by his Israelite birth mother, Moses was well aware of his Israelite heritage. One day, he saw an Egyptian beating an Israelite. Moses intervened, killing the

Egyptian. When Pharaoh heard of this, Moses fled for his life. Moses spent the next forty years becoming familiar with the desert as he shepherded small cattle, sheep, and goats.[10] Moses may have thought he would always be a shepherd. He did not know God was using this time in the desert as a training ground for the next stage in his life.

On what Moses thought to be an ordinary day, he saw a burning bush in the desert as he tended his flocks. According to Ronen Ben Moshe, an Israeli tour guide, a bush burning in the desert is not unusual. However, a burning bush not being consumed is quite unusual. "When the LORD saw that he turned aside to see, God called to him out of the bush, 'Moses, Moses!' And he said, 'Here I am'" (Exodus 3:4). Moses spoke only one Hebrew word, *hineini*, which means to be fully present.

Notice God did not speak to Moses until He captured his full attention.

Then God spoke.

In that order.

It makes me wonder how often I have been so preoccupied with going about my business that I did not notice God trying to gain my attention so He could speak to me.

Moses gave God his attention at once. However, his response to God's revelation, that he would be the one to lead the Israelites out of bondage in Egypt, was less than stellar. Moses was full of reasons (i.e., excuses) why he could not possibly do what God was asking him to do. God patiently addressed each of Moses' concerns right up until he asked God to send someone else. "Then the anger of the LORD was kindled against Moses" (Exodus 4:14).

Friend, believe me, this is not a position you want to be in. As a new Christian, I once said no to God. I cannot remember what He asked me to do. But I do remember that the weight of His displeasure was heavy. So heavy that when He called me to go on a mission trip to Kenya, I chose to go rather than ever feel that bad again. (This was at a time when I was dealing with chronic pain and could barely manage a trip to the grocery store.)

Instead of being excused from this service (as I guess Moses had hoped), God gave Moses an assistant—his brother Aaron. God also chose Aaron and his sons to be priests. This is the opposite of Korah's accusation when he said to Moses and Aaron, "Why then do you exalt yourselves above the assembly of the LORD?" (Numbers 16:3). Moses and Aaron did not choose the positions they were in. They were being obedient, serving in the positions God assigned to them.

Korah

Now let's turn our focus to Korah. When we met him in Numbers 16:1, we learned he was "the son of Izhar, son of Kohath, son of Levi." I noticed that he was the only person in this account who was given a genealogy this detailed. Everything in the Bible is there for a reason; every word contains significance. When we're given detailed information on one thing (or person) but not another, or when you read something in the Bible that stands out to you, it is important for us to ask the question, "Why do I need to know that?"[11]

When you read something in the Bible that stands out to you . . . ask the question, "Why do I need to know that?"

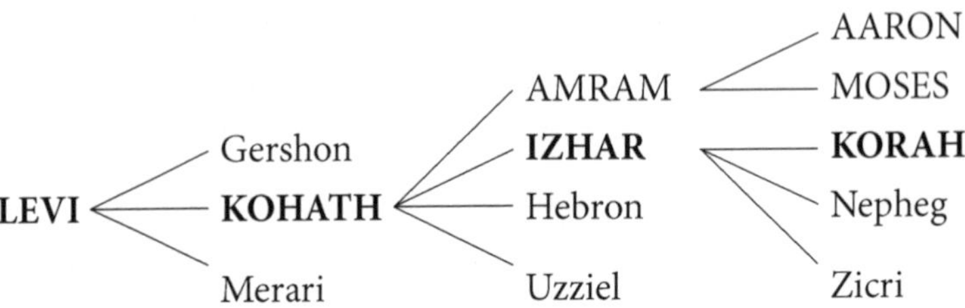

The information in Numbers 16:1 is printed in bold letters in the pedigree chart above. Using the genealogy of Levi found in Exodus 6:16–21, I filled in the family line of Kohath. Notice that Aaron, Moses, and Korah are all from the same generation. Their fathers are brothers and they have the same grandfather, Kohath. This means they are first cousins.

Did you have any idea Korah was so closely related to Moses and Aaron? I think it's safe to say that interaction with family members can be very different from dealing with anyone else. Imagine Korah's thoughts when he learned who was leading this group . . .

> *Moses? The pampered-in-the-palace Moses? He who lived in luxury while we worked as slaves Moses? The murderer Moses? The high-tail it and run so I don't have to face consequences Moses? The disappear to do who knows what for forty years Moses? What does he know about life as a slave? How can he possibly relate to us? What makes him think he is better than us? How is he qualified to be our leader? I am just as closely related to Levi as Moses is. Plus, I've never killed anyone!*

> We are often more critical of family members than we are of anyone else.

Before we're too critical of Korah, we need to think first about our own lives. Why is it that we are often more critical of family members than we are of anyone else . . . especially ourselves? While we cannot know Korah's thoughts, we do know he believed he, not Moses or Aaron, should be leading the nation of Israel. The problem for Korah is that leading this group of people was not Moses' idea. That directive came straight from God.

Digging Deeper

Can you think of a time when God spoke to you? How did you know it was God speaking?

Has God ever asked you to do something you knew you were not qualified to do? If so, what was it and what was your response?

Have you ever said no to God? If so, how did that work out?

Did you have any idea Korah was a first cousin to Moses and Aaron?

How does that relationship change how we look at this event?

Self-Discovery

What makes dealing with family members different from interacting with non-family?

Why do you think we tend to be more critical of family members than anyone else?

Chapter 4

The Timing

Under God's direction, Moses led the Israelites out of slavery in Egypt. As they traveled through the desert, his cousin Korah gathered some leaders and directed a rebellion against Moses and his brother Aaron. Being closely related, Korah may have thought he was just as qualified for the leadership positions as they were. I remind you of this because, up until this point, I have been laying the foundation for this study by answering the reporter's questions.[12] To gain a better understanding of a passage, ask the reporter's questions: Who? What? Where? Why? When? And How?

> To gain a better understanding of a passage, ask the reporter's questions: Who? What? Where? Why? When? And How?

That leaves us to determine *when* these events took place. The closest date recorded is found in Numbers 10:11–12. The Israelites had been camping at the base of Mount Sinai approximately fourteen months before God led them into the wilderness of Paran. There's no way of knowing exactly when Korah's rebellion took place after this, but there is another type of timeline we can follow.

After the Israelites refused to go into the Promised Land, God responded by saying, "None of the men who have seen my glory and my signs that I did in Egypt and in the wilderness, and yet have put me to the test these ten times and have not obeyed my voice, shall see the land that I swore to give to their fathers" (Numbers 14:22–23).

Did you catch that? This was not the first rebellion Moses had to deal with. It was at least the eleventh! Some scholars think the number ten was symbolic, indicating the nation rebelled numerous times. But the Talmud, a Jewish book of the Law,[13] actually lists ten specific incidents.[14]

The first occurred when the Israelites complained because they were trapped between Pharaoh and the Red Sea (Exodus 14:10-12). They were certain they were going to die. The next two rebellions were about the lack of water and food. In each of these cases, God provided. God gave them safe passage through the Red Sea and supplied the people with clean water to drink and manna to eat.

However, the Israelites then rebelled by not following the instructions given to them regarding manna. They attempted to keep it overnight (Exodus 16:19-20) and tried to collect it on the Sabbath (Exodus 16:26-28). They were told not to do either of these things. Here they faced what may be considered natural consequences. Kept overnight, the manna became full of maggots and began to smell. And when they looked for manna on the Sabbath, they found none.

> Thankful people are content people.

Following this, the Israelites again grumbled about the lack of water. And once again, God provided, this time bringing water from a rock (Exodus 17:1-7). While it is easy to be critical of the Israelite's behavior, it is important to recognize that up until this point, Israel was griping about the lack of necessities. Unfortunately, I know I have been guilty of grumbling about far less. One of the problems with grumbling is that it takes our focus off God's blessings. Thankful people are content people.

The real problems for Israel began while Moses was on Mount Sinai recording the laws God dictated. When Moses did not return in what the Israelites believed to be a timely manner, they asked Aaron to create new gods for them. Aaron did so, creating a golden calf that the people worshipped. They gave it the credit for rescuing them from slavery and oppression in Egypt. God had been patient up until this point, but now there were serious consequences for the Israelites. At God's command, around 3,000 of the rebellious men were killed that day (Exodus 32:1-29).

From this point on, the severity of the consequences continued to increase. Just after the nation of Israel set out after staying at Mount Sinai, they again grumbled. In response, God sent fire that consumed the outskirts of the camp. Despite this warning, in the very next verse we find them complaining again, this time about the lack of meat (Numbers 11:1-6).

In this instance, in addition to complaining, they also mourned the loss of their lives back in Egypt. "We remember the fish we ate in Egypt that cost nothing, the cucumbers, the melons, the leeks, the onions, and the garlic. But now our strength is dried up, and there is nothing at all but this manna to look at" (Numbers 11:5–6). Ah yes, the good old days when they were slaves making bricks without straw under the watch of harsh taskmasters. Seriously? No wonder God was furious!

God instructed Moses to tell the people,

> "Consecrate yourselves for tomorrow, and you shall eat meat, for you have wept in the hearing of the LORD, saying, 'Who will give us meat to eat? For it was better for us in Egypt.' Therefore the LORD will give you meat, and you shall eat. You shall not eat just one day, or two days, or five days, or ten days, or twenty days, but a whole month, until it comes out at your nostrils and becomes loathsome to you." (Numbers 11:18–20)

They wanted meat, so God gave them meat, along with another consequence.

> While the meat was yet between their teeth, before it was consumed, the anger of the LORD was kindled against the people, and the LORD struck down the people with a very great plague. Therefore, the name of that place was called Kibroth-hattaavah, because there they buried the people who had the craving. (Numbers 11:33–34)

Notice God did not kill people indiscriminately. It was the people crying out for meat who received the consequences.

This brings us to the tenth rebellion. This happened after twelve Israelite spies returned from scouting out the Promised Land. Because of the negative report from ten of the twelve spies,

> All the congregation raised a loud cry, and the people wept that night. And all the people of Israel grumbled against Moses and Aaron. The whole congregation said to them, "Would that we had died in the land of Egypt! Or would that we had died in this wilderness! Why is the LORD bringing us into this land, to fall by the sword?

> Our wives and our little ones will become a prey. Would it not be better for us to go back to Egypt?" And they said to one another, "Let us choose a leader and go back to Egypt." (Numbers 14:1–4)

In these four verses, we are told multiple times that the entire group, with the exception of Joshua and Caleb, refused to follow God into the Promised Land. As a result, God gave them exactly what they asked for. Every one of the adults who wished they would die in the wilderness would do just that. Aren't you glad God doesn't always give you what you want or what you deserve?

As you can see, Korah was not the first to rebel against authority; he was just one in a long line of complainers. If Israel was to survive in the desert, let alone become a nation and be an example to the world around them, the people had to be unified under their God-appointed leader, Moses.

Incident	Reference	Complaint/ Sin	Moses' Reaction	God's Response
1.	Exodus 14:10–29	Feared Pharaoh Doubted Moses & God	Reminded the people of God's promises.	Provided safe passage through the Red Sea.
2.	Exodus 15:22–26			

Incident	Reference	Complaint/ Sin	Moses' Reaction	God's Response
3.	Exodus 16:1–18			
4.	Exodus 16:19–26			
5.	Exodus 16:27–35			
6.	Exodus 17:1–7			

Incident	Reference	Complaint/ Sin	Moses' Reaction	God's Response
7.	Exodus 32:1–35	Created & worshipped golden calf, gave credit for their freedom to idol.	Sought God's favor, reminded God of His promises. Went down, broke tablets, enraged.	God's anger burned, threatened to destroy Israel. 3000 died, God sent a plague.
8.	Numbers 11:1–3			
9.	Numbers 11:4–34			
10.	Numbers 14:1–34	Feared entering Promised Land. Want to die/return to Egypt.	Fell facedown, reminded God of His promises, asked God to forgive Israelites.	Angry, forgave Israel. Granted their desire to die in the wilderness.

Digging Deeper

Fill in the blanks in the chart above (or use a separate piece of paper).

What did you learn about the Israelites?

What did you learn about Moses?

What did you learn about God?

What did you learn from this chart?

Self-Discovery

What is one thing you have been guilty of grumbling about lately?

List some positive things you can focus on instead:

Make a list of at least three things you are thankful for today.

Chapter 5

The Reubenites

It is important that we shift our focus as we study the Bible. Now that we have zoomed out and given Korah's rebellion some context, it is time to zoom back in[15] and return to the event itself. Zooming out (like a telescope) gives context, the big picture. Zooming in (like a microscope) helps us to focus on details.

Zooming out (like a telescope) gives context, the big picture. Zooming in (like a microscope) helps us to focus on details.

> Now Korah the son of Izhar, son of Kohath, son of Levi, and Dathan and Abiram the sons of Eliab, and On the son of Peleth, sons of Reuben, took men. And they rose up before Moses, with a number of the people of Israel, 250 chiefs of the congregation, chosen from the assembly, well-known men. They assembled themselves together against Moses and against Aaron

> and said to them, "You have gone too far! For all in the congregation are holy, every one of them, and the LORD is among them. Why then do you exalt yourselves above the assembly of the LORD?" (Numbers 16:1–3)

This was a serious offense, especially given the history of warnings and increasing consequences Israel received following past rebellions. Korah was not even the leader of his own clan, the Kohathites, yet he felt he was better qualified than Moses, Aaron, or anyone else when it came to leading the entire nation. Numbers 16:11 confirms that Korah had fallen into the Israelites detestable habit of grumbling. And as we have learned, God is not a fan.

Grumbling is contagious!

While studying this account of Korah's rebellion, we will discover multiple reasons why God is so angered by grumbling. In just these first three verses we see the first reason—grumbling is contagious. Think about it. When we are not content in our circumstances, we often look for someone to grumble to or commiserate with. Numbers 16:1 reveals that Korah was not alone in his cocky boldness. Three men from the tribe of Reuben—On, along with brothers Dathan and Abiram—became defiant as well. Why do you think they joined Korah's rebellion?

Another question is, how did the Reubenites become aware of this brewing dissent? I believe the much-neglected information found in Numbers chapters two and three gives us a clue. According to Numbers 2:10, the Reubenites were assigned to camp on the south side of the tabernacle. Also, "the clans of the sons of Kohath were to camp on the south side of the tabernacle, with Elizaphan the son of Uzziel as chief of the fathers' house of the clans of the Kohathites" (Numbers 3:29-30).

The tabernacle, the place where God dwelled among His people, was erected in the center of the camp. The Levites camped between the tabernacle and the rest of the nation, as a buffer of sorts. With both the Reubenites and the Kohathites camped on the south side of the tabernacle, this means they were neighbors. Do you think this camping arrangement may have contributed to the revolt?

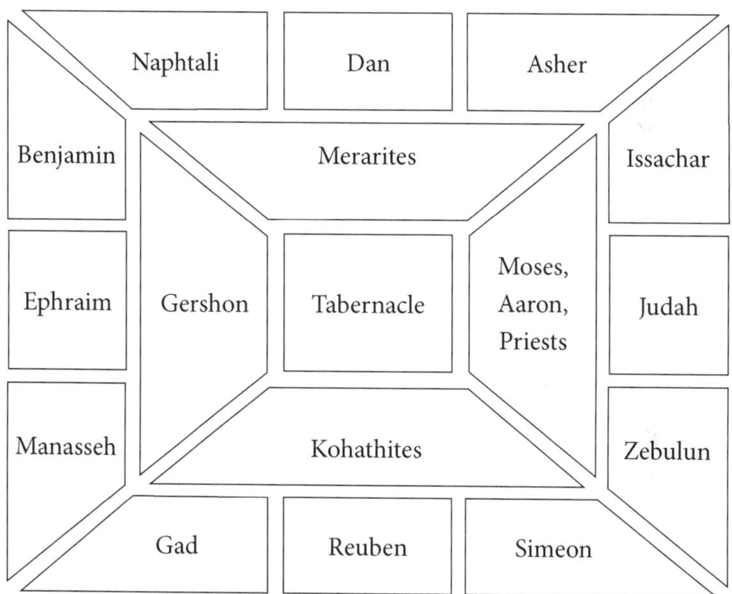

How easy would it have been for Korah to air his grievances to his neighbors the Reubenites and encourage them to follow suit? But notice, the conflict does not stop with the Reubenites. There were 250 community leaders (chiefs) who also jumped in on the rebellion (Numbers 16:2).

In Exodus 18 we find Moses sitting as judge and resolving disputes from morning until evening. His father-in-law suggests Moses

> "Look for able men from all the people, men who fear God, who are trustworthy and hate a bribe, and place

> such men over the people as chiefs of thousands, of hundreds, of fifties, and of tens. And let them judge the people at all times. Every great matter they shall bring to you, but any small matter they shall decide themselves. So it will be easier for you, and they will bear the burden with you. If you do this, God will direct you, you will be able to endure, and all this people also will go to their place in peace." (Exodus 18:21–23)

These chiefs were appointed to help bear Moses' burden and make his job easier. Yet it is 250 of these same leaders who joined Korah and the Reubenites in rebelling. Moses is God's chosen spokesperson, and the majority of his actions are in obedience to God's command. While it appears Moses selected these leaders, it was ultimately God who directed him in making these choices.

At the beginning of this book, I mentioned Numbers has a census both at the beginning and near the end of the book. While we generally associate a census with a long list of names, occasionally we find other little nuggets of truth. When we find anything that seems out of place in Scripture—such as anything other than names in a census—it is a signal that the information is important. For example, the census in Numbers 26 deviates from the list of names in verse nine to say, "Dathan and Abiram were the *community officials* who rebelled against Moses and Aaron and were among Korah's followers when they rebelled against the Lord" (NIV emphasis added).

When we find anything that seems out of place in Scripture . . . it is a signal that the information is important.

God interrupted the census to point out that Dathan and Abiram were among the men entrusted with leadership positions within the Israelite community. But rather than being grateful for the responsibility assigned to them, they wanted the authority Moses had. And Moses was the one who, at God's direction, gave them their leadership positions in the first place.

This grumbling spread like wildfire! The griping that originated with Korah spread first to Dathan and Abiram. They then aired their protests to their fellow community leaders. What started with one person spread to three people and then mushroomed into over 250!

This situation reminds me of a shampoo commercial televised in the 1980's. In it, the spokeswoman said the shampoo was so great that she told two friends about it. The screen then split into two pictures of her as she said, "and they told two friends," then split to four and finally sixteen shots of her as she continues, "and so on, and so on, and so on."[16]

That's how grumbling works, isn't it? We air our accusation to a few people, who each share it with a few people, and so on, and so on, and so on. Before you know it, you have full-out rebellion. Is it any wonder that God took swift action to put an end to this? Numbers 16:3 begins by saying, "They came as a group to oppose Moses" (NIV). Doesn't it sound like there was some planning involved here? Somewhere along the line this increasing grumbling turned to plotting and then matured to confrontation.

While no one is born content, the good news from Scripture is that we can learn to be content! By looking at where Korah went wrong, we can discover where we also may go wrong and determine the changes we need to make in our own lives. In applying these changes, one day we too can say, "I have learned to be content, whatever the circumstances" (Philippians 4:11 NIV).

Digging Deeper

Read Numbers 3:29–30. Who was in charge of the Kohathite clan?

Why do you think the three Reubenites joined in with Korah's rebellion?

Read Genesis 29:31–30:24 and 35:16-18. Near each name of the tribe leader in the camping illustration above, write the initial of his mother. L for Leah, R for Rachel, L(Z) for Leah's slave Zilpah, and R(B) for Rachel's slave Bilhah. What do you learn about the camping arrangement of the tribes?

Why do you think God organized the tribes in this way?

Self-Discovery

Describe a time you have experienced the spread of grumbling.

Think about a time when you grumbled. If you passed this complaint on to someone else, why do you think you did that?

In hindsight, what would have been a better option?

PART TWO

The Response

(Numbers 16:3–11)

Chapter 6

The Message

Korah is the ringleader of what is believed to be the eleventh rebellion of the Israelites. He was not happy with Moses, God's appointed leader. Korah shared his views with his neighbors, the Reubenites. They then complained to their fellow community leaders, and now the rebels numbered over 250. We have an idea of how this discontent spread, and we have looked at reasons why these leaders may have chosen to rebel, but there is one more thing to look at regarding the motivation behind this rebellion.

Look at the words Korah spoke to Moses and Aaron in Numbers 16:3, "You have gone too far! For all in the congregation are holy, every one of them, and the LORD is among them. Why then do you exalt yourselves above the assembly of the LORD?"

Where did Korah come up with this idea that every member of the group is holy? This is where knowing the context comes into play. Look at what we see when we back up and read the end of Numbers 15:

> The LORD said to Moses, "Speak to the Israelites and tell them that throughout their generations they are to make tassels for the corners of their garments, and put a blue cord on the tassel at each corner. These will serve as tassels for you to look at, so that you may remember all the LORD's commands and obey them and not become unfaithful by following your own heart and your own eyes. This way you will remember and obey all My commands and be *holy* to your God." (Numbers 15:37–40 HCSB emphasis added)

In the preceding verse, *holy* does not mean perfect. God knows that, as people who have been sinning since Adam and Eve, we are incapable of being holy apart from a savior. In fact, Jesus Himself says God is the only one who is even good (Matthew 19:17). The word *holy*, used in this context, means to be devoted to God and set apart for His specific use.[17] The Israelites are holy because God chose them and will use them to introduce the world to Him, the one true God.

Korah seems to be ignoring God's instruction "not to follow after your own heart and your own eyes" (Numbers 15:39) as he longs for the leadership roles of Moses and Aaron. He is also disobeying a few of God's commandments in the process.

Reading what comes before a passage in Scripture is one way to find the context. Another way is to utilize a tool known as a cross-reference.[18] The cross-reference in Numbers 16:3 refers us to Exodus 19:5–6: "Now therefore, if you will indeed obey my voice and keep my covenant, you shall be my treasured possession among all peoples, for all the earth is mine; and you shall be to me a kingdom of priests and a holy nation."

> Reading what comes before a passage in Scripture is one way to find context.

Again, notice there is a condition preceding God's promise: "*if* you will indeed obey my voice and keep my covenant" (Exodus 19:5). When Jesus died on the cross and rose from the dead, He paid the penalty for our sins. Thanks to Jesus, anyone who believes this and confesses their sin to God when they break one of His commandments or do things displeasing to Him, is indeed a member of His kingdom.[19]

Now let's turn our attention to Moses' response:

> When Moses heard it, he fell on his face, and he said to Korah and all his company, "In the morning the Lord will show who is his, and who is holy, and will bring him near to him. The one whom he chooses he will bring near to him. Do this: take censers, Korah and all his company; put fire in them and put incense on them before the Lord tomorrow, and the man whom the Lord chooses shall be the holy one. You have gone too far, sons of Levi!" (Numbers 16:4–7)

Verse four tells us Moses fell on his face. Did you ever stop to consider what that means? Moses performs this action three times in Numbers 16. This repetition points to its importance, so it is essential we understand why he has taken this position.

It is said that Scripture interprets Scripture, so we should first look to the Bible for answers rather than other sources. The phrase "fell on his face" appears multiple times in the Bible:

- God appeared to Abram in Genesis 17:1–3 and said, "'I am God Almighty; walk before me, and be blameless, that I may make my covenant between me and you, and may multiply you greatly.' Then Abram fell on his face."
- In Joshua 5:14, Joshua saw what appeared to be a man outside of Jericho, who introduced himself saying, "'I am the commander of the army of the Lord. Now I have come.' And Joshua fell on his face to the earth and worshiped."
- Joab, commander of King David's army, sent for a wise woman. In 2 Samuel 14:4 we're told "When the woman of Tekoa came to the king, she fell on her face to the ground and paid homage."

Falling facedown is often an act of reverence, though it was also "a common gesture of pleading in the ancient Near East. The physical position signifies that the one who bows is at the other person's mercy, since while in the position, the person could easily be killed."[20] Moses threw himself prostrate before God, showing humility despite the fact that Korah and his cohorts did not have the sense to do the same.

We aren't told how long Moses laid prone before God.

Imagine how uneasy the rebels and onlookers may have felt as they stood in silence, waiting for Moses to arise. What was God saying to Moses? What was Moses saying to God? I can think of a lot of things I would like to say (and probably have said) to God when I felt He placed me in a situation far above my abilities.

Finally, Moses stood. Then he spoke to the group.

First, in Numbers 16:5–7 Moses addressed Korah's accusation, informing him that God Himself will deal with the rebel's grab for power the next day. *Mahar* is the Hebrew word translated "tomorrow" in verse 7. *Mahar* "accompanies announcements of decisive acts of [God]; today is the day of preparation, *tomorrow* is the day of performance, action, or judgment."[21]

Did you notice that Moses ended the first part of his reply (verse 7) in exactly the same manner as Korah began his accusation (verse 3)? While Korah said Moses had gone too far, Moses turned that around and asserted it was Korah who had gone too far.

This phrase, "have gone too far," is a translation of just one Hebrew word, *rab.* It conveys the idea that the person spoken to "should go no further in a particular direction." *Rab* can also be translated "enough."[22] God speaks this word in Deuteronomy 1:6 and 2:3 when, after forty years of traveling, He says the Israelites have been in the desert long *enough.*

God also uses *rab* in Deuteronomy 3:26 when, to stop Moses' pleas to enter the Promised Land, He instructs Moses, "*Enough* from you; do not speak to me of this matter again" (emphasis added). So, Korah and Moses each directed this same word toward the other. It was as if they were each saying, "Enough! Step back from leadership at once! This nation needs to head in a different direction!"

Digging Deeper

Read Exodus 20:1–17. Which of the commandments do you feel Korah is *not* following?

NO other Gods before me
FALSE testomony
covet

Which commandment do you find to be the hardest to obey? Why?

Other Gods
IDOLS

Read Deuteronomy 3:23–27 and summarize what happened.

Moses wanted to enter into the promised land. But because the Lord was angry with him. The Lord did not allow it. He was allowed to see it from afar and strengthen Joshua to Lead

Read Mark 9:2–4. How does this passage connect to Deuteronomy 3:23–27?

TRANSFIGURATION
Moses shown promised land
from Mt. Pisgah

Self-Discovery

As a follower of Jesus, do you consider yourself to be holy according to the definition above? Yes/ set apart for the Lord

How does your life demonstrate that you are devoted to God?

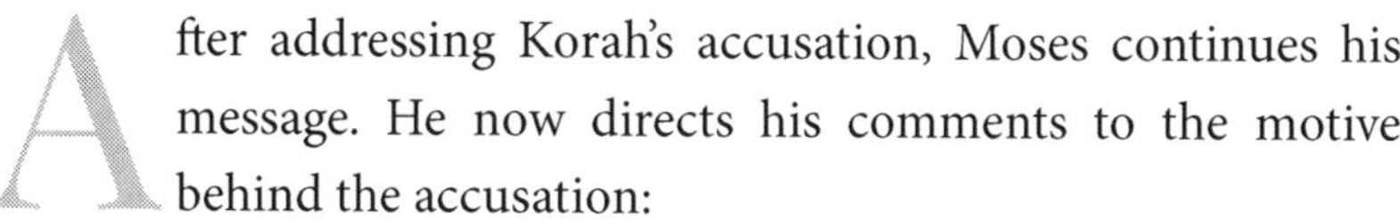

Chapter 7
The Motive

After addressing Korah's accusation, Moses continues his message. He now directs his comments to the motive behind the accusation:

> And Moses said to Korah, "Hear now, you sons of Levi: is it too small a thing for you that the God of Israel has separated you from the congregation of Israel, to bring you near to himself, to do service in the tabernacle of the LORD and to stand before the congregation to minister to them, and that he has brought you near him, and all your brothers the sons of Levi with you? And would you seek the priesthood also? Therefore it is against the LORD that you and all your company have gathered together. What is Aaron that you grumble against him?" (Numbers 16:8–11)

As a Levite, Korah enjoys the benefit of being separated out from the rest of the Israelites to serve God at the tabernacle. But Korah is not content with this privileged position. He has his eyes set on a loftier status. According to Moses, what Korah really wants is to be a priest, specifically the High Priest. Aaron's position.

The Levites are descendants of Jacob's son Levi. God appointed Aaron, a Levite, to be the High Priest. To qualify to be a priest, a man must be a descendant of Aaron. So, all priests are also Levites, but *only* the Levites descended from Aaron can be priests. This excludes Korah.

Numbers 16:9 tells us the Levites were separated from the rest of the Israelites. This separating took place earlier in their desert journey. Back in Exodus chapters twenty through twenty-four God verbally gave Moses the Ten Commandments and numerous other laws. Then "Moses came and told the people all the words of the LORD and all the rules. And all the people answered with one voice and said, 'All the words that the LORD has spoken we will do'" (Exodus 24:3).

After this positive affirmation from the Israelites, God then instructed Moses to come up on the mountain so He could give him the commandments written on tablets of stone. Moses spent forty days and forty nights there with God. Meanwhile, Aaron stayed behind to lead the people in Moses' absence. The Israelites said all the right words regarding obeying the covenant, but what would happen when it is time to put those words into practice?

If you recall from *Enough* chapter 4, in Moses' absence, the people persuaded Aaron to create an idol. "God had known all along what Moses had now learned the hard way—Aaron, the talented orator, would crumble in a crisis."[23] That idol was made in the form of a calf. In that culture a calf represented a "military figure who leads people into battle."[24] Now the Israelites had a visible (yet false) god to worship. Putting your trust in anything other than the one true God is called idolatry.

It was in the midst of this great sin that God ordered Moses back to the Israelites to deal with their disobedience:

> And as soon as he came near the camp and saw the calf and the dancing, Moses' anger burned hot, and he threw the tablets out of his hands and broke them at the foot of the mountain. He took the calf that they had made and burned it with fire and ground it to powder and scattered it on the water and made the people of Israel drink it. (Exodus 32:19–20)

Wait a minute! We know Moses has anger issues, but what is going on here? Reducing the golden calf to powder, adding water, and making the people drink it—that is weird! And yes, it is okay to say something in the Bible is weird. In fact, if it is weird, it is probably important![25]

If it is weird, it is probably important.

Since the creation of Adam and Eve, God instituted marriage to be between one man and one woman. This is to be an earthly reflection of God's relationship with His people. God is the bridegroom and those who believe in Him are His bride. The giving of the law on Mount Sinai was like a wedding. God viewed His relationship with the Israelites as a marriage, with the Ten Commandments being the wedding vows.[26]

Israel promised to be faithful to God, yet they created and worshipped an idol before Moses even had a chance to bring the tablets down from Mount Sinai. In today's culture, this would be like a bride having sex with a man other than the groom between the exchange of vows and the signing of the marriage license![27] Can you imagine how God felt about this?

Idolatry is a severe offense in God's eyes, but how does grinding up a burnt calf fit in? God is looking at Israel as a husband would an unfaithful wife. Did you know God made a provision in His law for a man who suspected his wife had been unfaithful? God made this provision in Numbers 5 to protect women against being divorced by their husbands based on a lie.

God directed the husband to bring his wife to the priest along with a grain offering. The priest placed some holy water into a clay jar along with some dust from the tabernacle floor. He wrote down the accusations against the wife, then rinsed the words off the page and into the water. The woman then drank it. If she was innocent nothing would happen to her. But if she was guilty there would be consequences.

At first glance, this ritual looks like pure superstition. But it is not. It is important to remember God wrote this law. He knows what is true and what is false. Moses is treating Israel's unfaithfulness according to God's law of jealousy. The ground up idol mixed in water did not merely represent the accusation against the people, it was the accusation! Just as an unfaithful wife had to pay the consequences if she sinned, so the guilty members among the Israelites would also face consequences:

> Moses saw that the people were running wild and that Aaron had let them get out of control and so become a laughingstock to their enemies. So he stood at the entrance to the camp and said, "Whoever is for the LORD, come to me." And all the Levites rallied to him.
>
> Then he said to them, "This is what the LORD, the God of Israel, says: 'Each man strap a sword to his side. Go back and forth through the camp from one end to the other, each killing his brother and friend and neighbor.'" The Levites did as Moses commanded, and that day about three thousand of the people died. Then

> Moses said, 'You have been set apart to the LORD today, for you were against your own sons and brothers, and he has blessed you this day.'" (Exodus 32:25–29 NIV)

From today's perspective this may seem like random violence, but we must remember God is never random. Knowing God's character, I don't think any innocent people were killed. I believe those who perished were the instigators and main participants in the idolatry. What do you think?

> **We must remember God is never random.**

Now we know why the Levites were set apart from the rest of the Israelites. They were the ones who came to Moses' aid when he asked who was for the Lord.

Digging Deeper

What is the difference between a priest and a Levite?

Priest were descended from Aaron

Levites from the tribe of Levi of which Aaron was.

Based on what we read in Exodus 32:19–29, describe how you think God feels about people worshipping idols.

Jealous God

Self-Discovery

While not many people worship little statues today in the United States, we still trust in things other than God. What or who do you have a tendency to put your trust in? Self - Husband, ability [illegible] so on.

What are some practical ways you can demonstrate that you trust God?

Every morning devotional and centering my life on God for that day and each moment that He leads me through relying on him prayerfully as a walk through.

Chapter 8

The Tabernacle

> And Moses said to Korah, "Hear now, you sons of Levi: is it too small a thing for you that the God of Israel has separated you from the congregation of Israel, to bring you near to Himself, to do service in the tabernacle of the LORD and to stand before the congregation to minister to them, and that he has brought you near him, and all your brothers the sons of Levi with you? And would you seek the priesthood also?" (Numbers 16:8–10)

If we look closely, we can see verse nine reveals four distinct privileges granted to the tribe of Levi. In the previous chapter we discovered why God separated the Levites from the rest of the tribes of Israel: they were the ones to answer the call when Moses asked who was for the Lord.

The next thing we learn from Numbers 16:9 is that God brought the Levites "near to himself." In the illustration of the Israelite's camping arrangements,[28] we found the Levites were located physically close to the tabernacle. They formed a ring of protection between the tabernacle in the center of camp, where God's presence dwelled, and the tents of the twelve tribes around the perimeter.

Then we are told the Levites are "to do service in the tabernacle of the LORD" (verse 9). We find details of this service in the first chapter of Numbers:

> "Appoint the Levites over the *tabernacle of the testimony*, and over all its furnishings, and over all that belongs to it. They are to carry the *tabernacle* and all its furnishings, and they shall take care of it and shall camp around the *tabernacle*. When the *tabernacle* is to set out, the Levites shall take it down, and when the *tabernacle* is to be pitched, the Levites shall set it up. And if any outsider comes near, he shall be put to death. The people of Israel shall pitch their tents by their companies, each man in his own camp and each man by his own standard. But the Levites shall camp around the *tabernacle of the testimony*, so that there may be no wrath on the congregation of the people of Israel. And the Levites shall keep guard over the *tabernacle of the testimony*." (Numbers 1:50–53 emphasis added)

Notice how often the word *tabernacle* is repeated in this passage. God uses repetition to emphasize something, so the tabernacle was obviously very important. That being the case, we should take a moment to learn what we can about it. Words are loaded with significance and meaning. To uncover the primary interpretation of a word, go back to the first time that word appears in Scripture.[29]

The Law of First Mention:
To uncover the primary interpretation of a word, go back to the first time that word appears in Scripture.

The first use of the term tabernacle is found in Exodus 25:8–9. God declares He will live among His people and will instruct them exactly how to create His "temporary housing."[30] The tabernacle was also referred to as the sanctuary or the tent of meeting. But why would God want a dwelling place? He's omnipresent (present everywhere) so He obviously does not need a place to stay. God knew the Israelites needed a constant reminder of His presence among them. To understand why, we must return to the early days of God's chosen people.

As we began our study, we discovered the nation of Israel originated when God invited Abraham into a relationship with Him. The bond between God and Abraham became so strong that Abraham was willing to sacrifice his son Isaac in obedience to God's command. But unfortunately, the faith of one generation is not automatically passed down to the next.

Despite Abraham's faithfulness to God, his grandson Jacob did not possess that same level of faith. Jacob left home and traveled to Paddan-aram where he married and had a large family. Jacob stayed there with his father-in-law Laban's family for twenty years before God called him to return, with his family, to his birthplace:

> So Jacob arose and set his sons and his wives on camels. He drove away all his livestock, all his property that he had gained, the livestock in his possession that he had acquired in Paddan-aram, to go to the land of Canaan to his father

> Isaac. Laban had gone to shear his sheep, and Rachel stole her father's household gods. (Genesis 31:17–19)

Did you catch that? Jacob's wife Rachel stole her father's idols! We do not know the depth of the idolatry in Jacob's family. Some scholars believe that some of Jacob's sons were even named after false gods![31] Genesis 31 reveals Laban in hot pursuit of his missing idols. When Laban finally catches up with his family members, he asks Jacob why he stole his gods. Jacob did not know anything about this and replied, "'Anyone with whom you find your gods shall not live . . .' Now Jacob did not know that Rachel had stolen them" (Genesis 31:32).

Laban searched the tents of Jacob and his wives to no avail, finally arriving at his daughter Rachel's tent. "Rachel had taken the household gods and put them in the camel's saddle and sat on them. Laban felt all about the tent, but did not find them. And she said to her father, 'Let not my lord be angry that I cannot rise before you, for the way of women is upon me'" (Genesis 31:34–35).

Every detail in Scripture is important. God often speaks in pictures, and here we see an illustration of exactly what God thinks of idols. *Where* were the idols placed? Underneath the filth of menstrual rags![32] Any connection to idols is detestable in God's eyes, and here we are given a visual image of that.

Every detail in Scripture is important!

In Genesis 35, God called Jacob to move to Bethel and make an altar to God there:

> So Jacob said to his household and to all who were with him, "Put away the foreign gods that are among you and purify yourselves and change your garments. Then let

> us arise and go up to Bethel, so that I may make there an altar to the God who answers me in the day of my distress and has been with me wherever I have gone." So they gave to Jacob all the foreign gods that they had, and the rings that were in their ears. Jacob hid them under the terebinth tree that was near Shechem." (Genesis 35:2–4)

What? I don't know which is harder to believe. Is it that members of Jacob's household were still carrying idols with them? Or that Jacob was aware of this? (He knew to instruct them to put away their idols.) Or that Jacob didn't destroy the idols but merely hid them? Even if we give Jacob's family the benefit of the doubt and assume they did leave their idols behind, when they later moved to Egypt, they found themselves right back in the heart of idolatry.

The Egyptians had many gods. Since the nation was so powerful and affluent, it appeared to them that the worship of these false gods was working. However, these gods were territorial. Each god's powers were limited to a certain geographic area. If someone moved to a different land, the first questions they would ask were "Which god is in charge of this new place?" and "What does this god want from me?" These gods were only responsible for certain things (god of the sun, god of the water, etc.) The idea of a God who was all powerful and ever present was a completely foreign concept to Jacob's descendants. Therefore, the Israelites had two questions on their minds as they followed Moses out into the desert:

#1. Is our God an all-purpose God?
#2. Will our God follow us out into the desert?[33]

This is why God instructed Moses to create the tabernacle. The Israelites would have a constant visual reminder of His presence. They needed to learn that God was the God of all things, and He would be with His people wherever they go. The book of Exodus ends with the completion of the tabernacle and God visibly taking up residence among His people:

> Then the cloud covered the tent of meeting, and the glory of the LORD filled the tabernacle. And Moses was not able to enter the tent of meeting because the cloud settled on it, and the glory of the LORD filled the tabernacle. Throughout all their journeys, whenever the cloud was taken up from over the tabernacle, the people of Israel would set out. But if the cloud was not taken up, then they did not set out till the day that it was taken up. For the cloud of the LORD was on the tabernacle by day, and fire was in it by night, in the sight of all the house of Israel throughout all their journeys. (Exodus 40:34–38)

Digging Deeper

Were you surprised to learn that Jacob's family carried idols with them? NO

Why do you think Jacob hid his family's idols rather than destroy them? Pressure from others in the family

~~perhap~~ maybe

If you remember, after refusing to enter into the Promised Land, the Israelites wished they had died in the desert. So God gave them what they said they wanted. Jacob makes an oath in Genesis 31:32: "Anyone with whom you find your gods shall not live." Read Genesis 35:16–19. Do you think there is a connection between Jacob's words and Rachel's death? DIFFICULT FOR me to

speculate

Self-Discovery

If your words became a reality, would you be happy with the outcome?

What an awesome responsibility our words are. Grateful to be able to repent and the grace, to change opportunity

List some ways that you can pass on your faith.

Chapter 9

The Move

We complete our look at Numbers 16:9 with one final piece of information about the responsibilities of the Levites. They were to minister to the congregation. The Bible uses repetition to draw our attention and to emphasize what is being said.[34] Notice the repetition in God's instructions regarding the Levites:

> The LORD spoke to Moses, saying, "Bring the tribe of Levi near, and set them before Aaron the priest, that they may minister to him. They shall keep guard over him and over the whole congregation before the tent of meeting, as they minister at the tabernacle. They shall guard all the furnishings of the tent of meeting, and keep guard over the people of Israel as they minister at the tabernacle. And you shall give the Levites to Aaron and his sons; they are wholly given to him from among the people of Israel." (Numbers 3:5–9)

> The Bible uses repetition to draw our attention and to emphasize what is being said.

The Levites are the guards over basically everything. They are to guard Aaron, the entire congregation, and everything in the tabernacle. They are also called to minister. The word *minister* in the Numbers 3:5–9 could also be translated as "serve." The Levites are called to serve the congregation, which is comprised of all the *ites* we discussed in *Enough* chapter 2. The Levites are also called to serve Aaron, and we are told the Levites are fully given to him.

I'm sure that went over well with Korah.

Much of the Levite's ministry to the congregation took place at the tabernacle. When the cloud representing the presence of God rose from above the tabernacle, the priests would sound the silver trumpets. This signaled to the nation of Israel that it was time to move to a new location. Each family was responsible for packing up their own tent and belongings. The Levites, however, did double duty. They were also responsible for the transportation of the tabernacle and all of its furnishings.

The tribe of Levi has three clans. Each clan is named after one of Levi's sons and contains that son's descendants. Each clan has specific responsibilities regarding the care and the transporting of the tabernacle. The Gershonites were responsible for the textiles belonging to the tabernacle—the tent, its coverings, curtains, etc. The Merarites were entrusted with the task of transporting and caring for the structure of the tabernacle—the frames, posts, bases, tent pegs, ropes, and so on. Korah's clan, the Kohathites, were responsible for transporting the most holy things.

I'm sure Korah enjoyed the prestige of being entrusted with the most holy things, but there was a catch. First, Aaron and the priests went in and prepared all the furnishings of the tabernacle to be moved:

> "When the camp is to set out, Aaron and his sons shall go in and take down the veil of the screen and cover the ark of the testimony with it. Then they shall put on it a covering of goatskin and spread on top of that a cloth all of blue, and shall put in its poles. And over the table of the bread of the Presence they shall spread a cloth of blue and put on it the plates, the dishes for incense, the bowls, and the flagons for the drink offering; the regular showbread also shall be on it. Then they shall spread over them a cloth of scarlet and cover the same with a covering of goatskin, and shall put in its poles." (Numbers 4:5–8)

Numbers 4 continues with more meticulous instructions detailing how each and every article in the tabernacle is to be prepared for the move. "And when Aaron and his sons have finished covering the sanctuary and all the furnishings of the sanctuary, as the camp sets out, after that the sons of Kohath shall come to carry these, but they must not touch the holy things, lest they die" (Numbers 4:15). I'm guessing Korah had a problem with that. He must move the holy things, but he cannot touch them.

When it came time to leave camp, the tribe of Judah led the procession. They were followed by the tribe of Issachar and then the tribe of Zebulun. Meanwhile, the Gershonites loaded the tabernacle's textiles on two carts that were pulled by four oxen. The Merarites filled their four wagons, pulled by eight oxen, and joined the Gershonites behind the tribe of Zebulun. This placement gave them time to set up the tabernacle and have it ready for the Kohathites when they arrived.

Next came the tribe of Reuben, the tribe of Simeon, and the tribe of Gad. The most holy articles, carried by the Kohathites, were safely nestled in the center of the caravan. The remaining six tribes followed. The articles from the tabernacle were too holy to be jostled around on a cart. Therefore, the Kohathites were not given any carts. "They were charged with the service of the holy things that had to be carried on the shoulder" (Numbers 7:9). That is why, after the layers of coverings were put in place, Aaron and his sons inserted carrying poles.

So, when it came time to move, Korah and his fellow Kohathites did not touch the most holy things. They merely grabbed on to the carrying poles, lifted the already covered items onto their shoulders and marched. I wonder if this was another bone of contention for Korah. After all, the other Levites were given carts to load and oxen to pull them. And they were able to actually touch what they were transporting.

But that is not all.

> The LORD spoke to Moses and Aaron, saying, "Let not the tribe of the clans of the Kohathites be destroyed from among the Levites, but deal thus with them, that they may live and not die when they come near to the most holy things: Aaron and his sons shall go in and appoint them each to his task and to his burden, but they shall not go in to look on the holy things even for a moment, lest they die." (Numbers 4:17–20)

Korah has to carry the most holy things, but he cannot touch them.

He cannot even look at them.

Even for a moment.

Or he will die.

But Aaron didn't have to carry anything on his shoulders. He sees these items. He works with them. He touches many of them on a regular basis. Korah does not see God is protecting him by having Aaron prepare the articles for moving. Korah is only focused on what he does not have and cannot do. His comparison leads to discontent.

Comparison leads to discontent.

Korah wants the tables to be turned.

Korah wants to be Aaron.

Korah's inability to touch and see the most holy things may seem harsh and unfair. But God applied these restrictions to everyone except the priests, whose duties included working with these items. And even the priests would die if they looked in the Most Holy Place to view the ark. Only Aaron, the high priest, was allowed in there, and that was only once a year on the Day of Atonement.

We do not think the power company is harsh and unfair when they forbid us from touching a downed power line. We understand that exposure to that level of power is deadly. I think one of the reasons the most holy items are dangerous is because they contain God's power. It is only through the blood of Jesus that we are able to come near to God and live.

When I think about Korah's attitude toward Moses and Aaron, the childhood chant, "You're not the boss of me!" comes to mind. Sorry to break it to you Korah, but according to God, Aaron *is* the boss of you. And I think that is one reason why Korah rebelled. I believe he wanted Aaron to be serving him, not the other way around.

Korah was stuck in an Egyptian mindset. Back in Egypt (and in our world today), the people in the top positions ruled. Everyone had to do what Pharaoh said . . . or else! In God's kingdom, the people in the top positions are called to serve. That is why Jesus spoke such harsh words to the religious leaders of His day. Those in the positions closest to God were supposed to be reaching out and ministering to the people on the fringes. Instead, they were consumed with wealth, power, and status. They kept the outsiders away from their domain rather than welcoming them in and pointing them to God.

As children of God, we are called to serve. The question is, how am I serving? Am I doing so joyfully, knowing that all servants of God are valued by Him? Or am I serving like Korah, focusing not on God, but on what I do not have?

Digging Deeper

List the words you find repeated in Numbers 3:5–9.

Tabernacle work

Give levites to aaron

Why do you think these words are emphasized?

Self-Discovery

Are you serving God, content in the position He has chosen for you at this time? Or are you serving like Korah, focusing not on God, but on what you don't have? I realize I am on reliance of God that through him I can do all things through him who strengthens me

If you are serving like Korah, list some ways you can change your focus. good to remain under prayer-ful examination

Can you think of a time when God protected you, but you did not realize it until after the fact? If so, please describe it below.

many -

Chapter 10

The Grumbling

As we discovered in the previous chapter, Korah's problem stemmed from the fact that his focus was on what he did not have. I believe this is a major reason why Korah was not content with his position. He wanted more. It is not any easier to be content today. There is an entire industry determined to keep us focused on what we do not have. It is estimated that more than 700 billion dollars was spent on advertising globally in 2022. Three hundred billion of that was spent in the United States alone.[35]

Advertising comes in many forms. Every spring and fall the Home Builders Association in our community hosts "The Parade of Homes" in hopes of selling goods and services. An affordable ticket allows you to enter more than one hundred newly built homes over a span of three weekends. These houses are fitted with the latest and greatest appliances and furnishings. They smell of fresh paint and newly laid carpet.

When I was younger, returning to my modest home after visiting the Parade was always a let-down. It felt like I returned to a hovel after touring these lavish homes. There was nothing wrong with the house I was living in, but I was only looking up the ladder, comparing my house to homes few people could afford to own.

At that time, I never gave a thought to those who had less than me.

It does not appear that Korah did either.

Moses lists the privileges of Korah and his fellow Levites. He is well aware that what Korah really wants is to be the high priest, a job that already belongs to Aaron. Now he concludes his comments to Korah saying, "It is against the LORD that you and all your company have gathered together. What is Aaron that you grumble against him?" (Numbers 16:11).

Moses finishes his response to Korah's accusations by informing him who he is really opposing: God! Korah complained about both Moses and Aaron, but God was the one who placed them in these positions. When we grumble against someone in authority over us, we too are actually rebelling against God.

Korah was grumbling, but what exactly does that entail? The word grumble is also translated as "complain about" or "murmur" in other versions of the Bible. Sometimes an ordinary dictionary can be helpful in understanding the words of Scripture. While these words are all similar in the English language, there are subtle differences between the three.

An ordinary dictionary can be helpful in understanding the words of Scripture.

Grumble: "to murmur or mutter in discontent; complain sullenly."[36]

Murmur: "a low, continuous sound . . . a mumbled or private expression of discontent."[37]

Complain: "to express dissatisfaction, pain, uneasiness, censure, resentment, or grief; find fault . . . to make a formal accusation."[38]

Grumbling is more serious than one might think. In the Bible, the word translated as "grumble" is the Hebrew word *lun* (pronounced "loon"). *Lun* can literally mean to stay put. It has a broader meaning of *kvetching*, a Yiddish word that means to "complain persistently and whiningly."[39]

Korah is not just *kvetching*, but also murmuring and pushing back. There is an attitude of complaining with a resistance to it. That is why *lun* is translated as "grumble against." Korah is stating he will no longer follow Moses and Aaron's leadership. "And that is the part that angers God. It is not just the *kvetching*; it is that they are not going to go any farther. They are not going to follow God anymore because He has to prove Himself first."[40]

Korah is breaking a very important command: Do. Not. Test. God.

This is a lesson that Korah and his cohorts should have already learned. Back in Exodus 17, the Israelites camped at Rephidim. "But the people thirsted there for water, and the people grumbled (*lun*) against Moses and said, 'Why did you bring us up out of Egypt, to kill us and our children and our livestock with thirst?'" (Exodus 17:3).

The Israelites had a legitimate need. Clean drinking water is a necessity, especially when traveling in the desert. But they were doing more than voicing a need. They were implying that their lives would be better if they had remained slaves in Egypt. They also accused Moses of bringing them out into the desert to kill them! Still, God provided water for them—from a rock of all places. Moses "called the name of the place Massah (to put someone to the test) and Meribah (place of strife), because of the quarreling of the people of Israel, and because they tested the Lord by saying, 'Is the Lord among us or not?'" (Exodus 17:7).

Of course, the Lord was among them. They were *not* merely wandering. God was *leading* the Israelites through the desert, every step of the way. The tabernacle was a visual reminder of this.

In the hierarchy of Israelite leadership, God is unquestionably at the top. Since God chose to speak to and through Moses, I placed him next in the chain of command. As high priest, Aaron came after Moses. Aaron was followed by his two sons, the priests. I would put the Kohathites next since they transport the most holy furnishings of the tabernacle. The Gershonites and Merarites would come after them, followed by the twelve tribes of Israel. Then, of course, there are the non-Israelites that were traveling with them, plus the rest of the world.

God
Moses
Aaron, high priest
Eleazer and Ithamar, priests
Korah and his fellow Kohathites
Gershonites and Merarites
The twelve tribes
The non-Israelites who left Egypt with them
The rest of the world

Do you see what was happening? The Kohathites could count on one hand the number of people who had greater access to God than they did. One hand! Yet Korah and his cohorts wanted more. In evaluating their position, the rebels were only looking up the ladder at those who had what they desired. They did not bother looking down the ladder at the rest of the world's population. Grumbling is the product of looking up to those who have more instead of looking down to the less fortunate.

Grumbling is the product of looking up to those who have more instead of looking down to the less fortunate.

Decades after my "Parade of Homes" experience, God sent me to Kenya. I stood by a woman on the dirt floor of her newly built, two-room home. She knelt, surrounded by freshly packed mud walls in a house that would easily fit in one half of a two-stall garage. As she knelt, she wept.

But she did not weep because the tin roof over her head was flimsy. She did not weep because her home was not as large as those belonging to the community leaders. Or because her home was not made of brick like theirs were. Speaking through an interpreter between sobs, she revealed her reason for weeping:

It was because she never thought she would have a house THIS NICE!

This woman demonstrated the joy of thanksgiving that pleases God. She wept in gratitude over God's provision for her rather than focus on what others had. She was thankful for solid walls that would not cave in on her children. She appreciated the tin roof, which would not attract insects nor allow water to drip on her family when the rainy season came.

One of the reasons God hates our grumbling is because our focus is not on Him and the many ways He blesses us. Instead, our focus is on what we do not have. One of the lessons that stood out to me from a study I did early on in my walk with Jesus was this: "What we focus on gets bigger."[41]

Not only does what we focus on get bigger, what we focus on is a *choice*! We can keep our focus on what we do not have, or we can choose to focus on what we do have and the many ways God has blessed us.

Which are you choosing today?

Digging Deeper

In your own words, describe the differences between grumbling, murmuring, and complaining.

grumbling - expressing ~~annoyance~~ dissatisfaction in a bad tempered way.

~~sub~~ subdue of dissatisfaction or discontent. complaining annoyance about something

Which word best describes you when you are upset?

Self-Discovery

We often think that the Israelites were wandering in the desert, but the truth is they were being led. How can we apply this truth to our own lives? Daily centering on God through Bible, Prayer, other Religious books

Has it ever occurred to you that your grumbling is actually against God? Yes

What would be a better way to deal with those feelings?

Prayerfully bring them before the Lord

1 - 31 - 2024

CORA - yrs old

KAI - 14 years old - Heart + Lungs OK.

Kelly & Nick Burry parents

CAROL - Norologist appt.

FRAN - A-FIB on 2-12-2024

PART THREE

The Reubenites

(Numbers 16:12–17)

Chapter 11

Dathan and Abiram

After delivering his response to Korah's accusations, Moses now turns to hear from his cohorts, Dathan and Abiram. We previously explored the possibility that these Reubenites may have caught Korah's attitude of discontent while camping near him. But it also appears there could be two rebellions occurring simultaneously. Korah is envious of Aaron and wants the priesthood, but the Reubenites' beef is primarily with Moses. Korah wants to be the spiritual leader while Dathan and Abiram want to be political leaders.

The Bible tells us sin and its consequences can be passed down through generations.[42] The tribe of Reuben is living with consequences from the sin of their namesake, the son of Jacob. I wonder if God was thinking specifically of Jacob when he dictated Deuteronomy 21:15–17 to Moses. It speaks of the exact situation Jacob found himself in. He had one wife (Rachel) whom he loved, and another wife (Leah) whom he did not love. These verses specify that the firstborn son is to receive a portion of the father's inheritance that is double that of the other sons. This applies even if the first son was born to the unloved wife, as Reuben was.

As the eldest son, Reuben was left in charge in his father's absence. But after Rachel's death, Reuben slept with Bilhah, his father's concubine. This action broke God's law and could have cost Reuben his life.[43] After this insult to his father, Reuben lost the privileges that would have been his as the firstborn. Instead, they went to Joseph, the firstborn son of Jacob's favorite wife Rachel. This is reflected in the list of the tribes of Israel in Numbers 13. Ephraim and Manasseh, sons of Joseph, each were leaders of a tribe, giving Joseph a double portion. Not Reuben.

As the tribes followed God's presence through the wilderness, they were led by the tribe of Judah. Perhaps the Reubenites jumped on the "oppose Moses" bandwagon because they felt, as descendants of Jacob's firstborn son, they should be first in line as they followed God through the desert. Instead, they found themselves marching fourth, behind three tribes plus two clans of Levites. Or, they may have felt entitled to Moses' position because he was descended from Jacob and Leah's third son, Levi.

> And Moses sent to call Dathan and Abiram the sons of Eliab, and they said, "We will not come up. Is it a small thing that you have brought us up out of a land flowing with milk and honey, to kill us in the wilderness, that you must also make yourself a prince over us? Moreover, you have not brought us into a land flowing with milk and honey, nor given us inheritance of fields and vineyards. Will you put out the eyes of these men? We will not come up." And Moses was very angry and said to the LORD, "Do not respect their offering. I have not taken one donkey from them, and I have not harmed one of them." (Numbers 16:12–15)

Wow! Moses gives Dathan and Abiram an opportunity to air their complaints, but they refuse to meet with him. Why? Are they afraid, or maybe ashamed, to speak these traitorous words directly to Moses? If only they had that much sense. Their accusations are hemmed in by the phrase, "We will not come up." Initially I thought this was just a refusal to meet Moses, but it is actually more than that.

In the Bible, "come up" is the translation of the Hebrew word *alah*, which can mean to approach someone in authority.[44] This is seen in Deuteronomy 25:7, where a wife who has been wronged is directed to "*go up* to the gate to the elders" (emphasis added). In the time when judges led the nation of Israel, Deborah sat under a palm tree "in the hill country of Ephraim, and the people of Israel *came up* to her for judgment" (Judges 4:5 emphasis added). Dathan and Abiram's use of the words "come up" make it clear not only that they will not be honoring Moses' request, but also that they will no longer acknowledge him as their leader.

In the previous chapters, we took a close look at the list of God-given benefits Moses pointed out to the Kohathites. We should always be on the lookout for lists as we read Scripture. In the verses from Numbers 16 above, we see another list. Here the Reubenites, Dathan and Abiram, respond to Moses with a list of their own.

Be on the lookout for lists as we read Scripture.

Notice the details of Moses' alleged offenses listed in verses 13–14:

1. You brought us out of a land of milk and honey.
2. You brought us into the wilderness to kill us.
3. You made yourself a prince over us.
4. You have not brought us into a land of milk and honey, fields and vineyards.

This list is full of twisted facts and exaggerations. Let's address the first of these accusations.

The phrase "land flowing with milk and honey" first appears in Exodus 3:8. God, speaking through the burning bush, informs Moses He will bring the Israelites out of the land of Egypt and into "a land flowing with milk and honey, to the place of the Canaanites." Let's look at this literally. Milk comes from grazing animals such as cows and goats. Honey comes from bees, which need blooming plants to gather nectar. So, a land flowing with milk and honey is a fertile land, capable of supporting fields and wildlife.

The phrase, "land flowing with milk and honey," is found many times in the Bible, including the account of the previous rebellion in Numbers 13–14. When the Israelites first reached Canaan, they sent twelve spies into the land, one man from each tribe. After forty days the men returned with their report. Two spies had a positive message. The Promised Land was indeed a land of milk and honey, just as God described. They returned with pomegranates, figs, and one cluster of grapes so large it was carried on a pole between two men! But the other ten spies only spoke of the giants who lived there, instilling fear into the rest of the nation. Unfortunately, the majority of Israelites refused to enter the land. They feared its inhabitants rather than trusting God for protection and victory.

The only time this phrase is not referring to Canaan is here, in Numbers 16:13, where Egypt is described as such a wonderful land. Egypt! The nation that kept the Israelites slaves for the previous 400 years. "That Dathan and Abiram would use the common description for Canaan to describe Egypt shows the seriousness of their rebellion."[45]

> Part of being content is owning your decisions.

Part of being content is owning your decisions. The account of the previous rebellion in Numbers 14 shows the Reubenites are not doing this. Dathan and Abiram were part of the problem. They were among those who refused to enter the Promised Land. They joined in the chorus saying they would rather have died in Egypt or in the desert. They wanted to go back to the land of slavery. They even considered stoning Moses! The truth is, *they* are responsible for the fact that they are not leadership material. They are not even good followers. Why would they think they were capable of leading?

You will never find contentment if you believe it depends on the actions of other people.

Digging Deeper

Why do you think the Reubenites felt they should be leading Israel?

because of the Laws of First born.

Reread Numbers 16:12–15. Who really did the things the Reubenites are crediting to Moses?

The Lord brought them out

What difference does that make?

~~the~~ Because the Lord brought them out of Egypt his motives are perfect.

Self-Discovery

There is never an acceptable time to ignore God or disobey His summons. When have you tuned God out or disobeyed Him?

What were the consequences?

Do you consider yourself to be a good follower? If so, why?

Chapter 12

The List

Let's review our look at the grievances the Reubenites leveled against Moses in Numbers 16:13–14:

1. You brought us out of a land of milk and honey.
2. You brought us into the wilderness to kill us.
3. You made yourself a prince over us.
4. You have not brought us into a land of milk and honey, fields and vineyards.

Life in the desert is difficult, and these Reubenites are placing all of the blame squarely on Moses. Looking back with their rose-colored glasses, Dathan and Abiram seem to have forgotten they were slaves in Egypt. Now they are accusing Moses of intentionally trying to kill them. On multiple occasions, Moses heard the people claim they were better off dead. These accusations started before the Israelites even crossed through the Red Sea.

The nation of Israel was seemingly trapped. The Red Sea was ahead of them, and Pharaoh's army was closing in from behind. Rather than turning to God and asking for His help, the Israelites turned to blame Moses. It appears the thought of God intervening never occurred to them. So they accusingly asked Moses if he brought them into the desert to die because there were no graves in Egypt. It is funny if you think about it. The pyramids are evidence that, if the Egyptians had one thing, it was graves.

In the previous rebellion, the Israelites refused to enter the Promised Land. They said it would be better to die in the desert than face the enemy currently living in the land. That seems to be their go-to response. We should pay attention to patterns of behavior. I can picture them, each flinging the back of their hand against their forehead, saying "If only we would have died . . . " every time they faced hardship. Now the Reubenites seem to be taking it up a notch. It was bad enough when they repeatedly said they would be better off dead. Now they are accusing Moses of trying to kill them!

Pay attention to patterns of behavior.

This accusation against Moses is absurd. The Israelites assume he has evil intentions, deliberately trying to kill them. In truth, Moses saved them from death a number of times. He spoke to God on their behalf. Even when God threatened to abandon the Israelites and make Moses into an even greater nation, Moses reminded God of the promise He made to deliver the Israelites. How easy would it have been for Moses to instead say, "You are right God. These people are hopeless! Let's start over again. I'm sure my descendants will be more obedient than these people are."

In their third accusation, Dathan and Abiram say Moses wants to be a prince over them. This reminds me of an event that happened when I was a new Christian. I volunteered to help at a funeral luncheon at my church. Working in the kitchen alongside seemingly mature women of faith, I assumed they had it all together.

Cora was clearly in charge, assigning the rest of us to the various tasks. I was unaware of any discord until it came time to clean up. I was standing next to Martha, a woman near my mother's age. As Cora passed by, Martha uttered a phrase I had never heard before. She commented, under her breath, "I wonder who died and made her queen?" Alas, competition was alive and well in the church kitchen. Why do we have such a hard time submitting to those in authority over us? Or to others in general?

I wonder if Dathan and Abiram, like Martha, chafed at the idea of someone they saw as an equal putting themselves in a leadership role. Except, of course, for the fact that Moses did not place himself in the role of leadership over the Israelites. "[Moses] was sent to be their ruler and deliverer by God himself, through the angel who appeared to him in the bush" (Acts 7:35 NIV). When God placed him in charge, Moses did not jump at the opportunity. Instead, he tried to get out of it. The truth was the opposite of the Reubenites accusation.

While being adopted by Pharaoh's daughter may have literally made Moses a prince, Dathan and Abiram accused him of making himself a prince. Interestingly, the same statement was made back in Egypt. Moses killed an Egyptian man who abused an Israelite slave. The following day he saw two Israelites fighting with each other. When he intervened, the man in the wrong said, "'Who made you a prince and a judge over us? Do you mean to kill me as you killed the Egyptian?'" (Exodus 2:14).

After taking Moses out of Egypt, God spent the next forty years taking Egypt out of Moses.

Once Pharaoh heard about this incident, Moses ran for his life. After taking Moses out of Egypt, God spent the next forty years taking Egypt out of Moses. And because of the previous rebellion,

God will spend another forty years removing the Egyptian mindset from the Israelites.

Have you ever considered what the transition from prince to shepherd was like for Moses? Change is never easy. He was raised in a palace, with servants to tend to his every need. Suddenly he finds himself herding sheep in the desert. To say he was ill-equipped for this position would be an understatement. The man pampered and perfumed in the palace was now sleeping on the ground with smelly sheep. I think the conversion was a challenging one. Moses' choice of name for his firstborn son is telling. He called him Gershom, which can mean "wanderer there," or "expelled one."[46]

I find the final accusation the most brazen. Moses is accused of not bringing the nation into a land flowing with milk and honey. Of not bringing them the wealth and prosperity that comes from owning fields and vineyards.[47] That may be technically true, for Moses did not bring the Israelites *into* the Promised Land. But the fact is Moses did lead them *to* the Promised Land. Have they so quickly forgotten they were among the people refusing to enter it?

We began by viewing the Reubenites list of accusations against Moses. Let's conclude with a refreshing look at the truth:

- God is the One who led the Israelites out of Egypt—the land of slavery and oppression.
- God is the One who led them into the wilderness. He did not do it to kill them, but to save them. They are the ones who want to die in the desert. God will merely grant their request.
- God is the One who appointed a reluctant Moses to lead His people.
- God is the One who led them to the Promised Land. They are the ones who refused to enter.

Before we look to blame someone else, we must first examine ourselves.

When life gets difficult or something goes wrong, where do you turn? Do you look to God? Do you examine yourself? Or do you turn to find someone to blame as the Reubenites did? God is the only One who knows every detail about you and every detail about your situation. While it is sometimes wise to ask another person for insight, that should never be our first response. God is the one we should go to first. And before we look to blame someone else, we must first examine ourselves and ask God to show us what we may be blind to.

Digging Deeper

Read Exodus 14:13–14. Can you think of a situation where you need God to fight for you? If you haven't already, ask Him for His help.

Self-Discovery

Have you ever been falsely accused of something or had your motives distorted? How did you respond?

Why do you think we have such a hard time submitting to those in authority over us?

Have you ever experienced a difficult transition in your life? If so, what did you learn from the process?

Can you think of a behavior, habit, or mindset you need God to transform? If not, ask Him to show you what you need to change to be more like Him. Then ask Him to guide you through the process.

Chapter 13

The Ghosting

Dathan and Abiram finish their critique of Moses' leadership, complete with false accusations and revisionist history. They are blind to the fact that they only have themselves to blame for the situation they are in. Their unseeing eyes refuse to recognize that rebellions like this are part of the reason they are not already in the Promised Land. Yet they dare say to Moses, "Will you put out the eyes of these men?" (Numbers 16:14).

War is a savage business. In those days, it was not uncommon to literally remove the eyes of an enemy to render them harmless.[48] We see this in Judges 16:21, where the Philistines gouged out Samson's eyes after his capture. Runaway slaves also risked having their eyes gouged out.[49] However, in this situation, it is thought that the statement is a figurative one. Dathan and Abiram are hinting that Moses is demanding blind obedience from them.[50]

Also, when Dathan and Abiram speak of putting out the eyes of "these men," they are actually referring to themselves. At that time, harm was never spoken of oneself. Instead it was diverted on to a third person.[51] They are, in fact, accusing Moses of misleading them.

I love the way this Old English version puts it: "'Dost thou think so absolutely to blind us, that none of us shall discern thy craft and ambition. Do you think you will be able to hoodwink us and lead us around like blind men under pretense of bringing us to a rich and fertile country?' The Reubenites were blinded by discontented, proud and rebellious spirits."[52]

Grumbling leads to disobedience.

After their snub, they end their statement the same way it began. They again refuse to come to Moses as he requested. Their grumbling leads to disobedience.

Not surprisingly, Moses is exasperated. Not only are Dathan and Abiram rebelling against his leadership, but now they are also refusing any direct communication. Today we would say these Reubenites were "ghosting" Moses—refusing to communicate without any explanation. Personally, I cannot think of anything I find more frustrating. Or more immature. These Reubenites have their say and then refuse any further discussion.

"Then Moses became very angry and said to the LORD, 'Do not accept their offering. I have not taken so much as a donkey from them, nor have I wronged any of them'" (Numbers 16:15 NIV).

We can learn a lot by comparing and contrasting parts of Scripture. As we looked at Dathan and Abiram, we saw them twisting the facts, exaggerating, and outright lying. They assumed they knew Moses' intentions and accused him of leading them into the desert to kill them. They aimed their grievances at Moses but did not even show him the courtesy of speaking to him directly. Instead, their words were delivered to Moses through some unfortunate messenger.

> We can learn a lot by comparing and contrasting parts of Scripture.

Grumbling and complaining are often used as synonyms, but they are actually two very different actions.[53] Dathan and Abiram grumbled. They spoke words that were not true. They made false accusations. They were prideful. They did not take responsibility for their own actions but turned to blame someone else.

In contrast, Moses complained. He was angry, but being angry is not a sin. Leaders are human and even the most patient have their limits. Moses was honest. He owned his feelings and spoke the truth. We know he had the habit of humbling himself before God, and he spoke to Him directly. He did not make assumptions or false accusations. While Dathan and Abiram were focused only on themselves, Moses was concerned for the good of the entire nation. We all have our moments of grumbling to and about others, but this is not pleasing to God. Instead, God invites us to bring our complaints to Him.

At the end of my first day in Kenya, I felt I had a lot to complain about. Despite a grueling twenty-four hours of travel, I found myself sleepless in our Nairobi guest house. In the morning, our group was shuttled to a small airport and loaded into a tiny airplane. Aloft, I learned that I *do* get airsick. At least I do while flying in a rainstorm, with the plane being tossed to and fro like clothing in a washing machine.

I prayed through the seemingly endless flight. We finally landed on the island in Lake Victoria on our second attempt. (The first was a deliberate miss as we buzzed the so-called runway to drive off the grazing cattle. This did not help my nausea. At all.) While I desired to kiss the ground after disembarking, I instead chose to walk along the runway. My hope was to conquer my queasy stomach, rather than being sick in front of a large crowd of curious schoolchildren watching our every move.

I hadn't made it far when I was given some distressing news.

We were not at our final destination.

We needed to board a small boat.

Immediately.

Fantastic.

With my eyes fixed on the horizon, I was able to keep the remaining contents of my stomach intact. Our small boat landed a few miles down the shore, but all I could see was a tall row of shrubs. As I walked through the small opening in the center, my heart sank. Before me was a field of tents.

And not the kind of tents that have beds in them.

After attempting to eat a dinner that was looking back at me, my husband escorted me up the dark hill to the latrine. Along the way I stepped in a hole and jammed my hip—a repeat of an injury that occurred just days before our departure and left me barely able to stand up straight, let alone move.

That was the last straw!

My husband escorted me back to our pup tent, after which he conveniently (and wisely) escaped. I proceeded to have it out with God. Listing the events of the day, I told Him exactly how I felt. I ended my rant by saying, "And if I knew I wouldn't have a bed I never would have come!" To which God replied loud and clear (though not audibly), "I know. That is why I did not tell you."

At the end of what may arguably be the most difficult day of my life, I could do nothing but laugh! God knows me so well. He blinded me to the fact that I would not be sleeping on a bed because He knew that would be the one thing that would keep me from being obedient to Him.

In this instance, when I accused my husband of bringing me to Kenya to kill me, I was grumbling. But when I poured out my heart honestly to God, I was complaining. And God is big enough to handle all our complaints. God does not want us grumbling to those around us. He invites us to come to Him with all of our concerns.

Where do you turn when you are upset or overwhelmed?

Digging Deeper

Read Ephesians 4:26–27. Describe a time when you were angry but did not sin. Or perhaps a time when you did sin in your anger. If the latter, how could you have responded differently?

Be angry but do not let the sun go down on your anger

my mom saying this verse to me as a child of around 7-8 as she was putting me to bed. Don't remember the incident but clearly remember her saying this and praying w/me. It's something that has stayed with me throughout my life

Self-Discovery

When have you found yourself blind to something?

Do you tend to grumble when you're upset or overwhelmed, or do you complain?

Have you ever been "ghosted?" If so, how did you respond?

No, but I think I would find it ver

disconcerting.

Can you think of a time when you ghosted God? Why did you stop communicating with Him? Good Question.

Fodar for thought

Chapter 14

The Request

Moses' stomach is in knots. It is bad enough he is dealing with yet another rebellion. But now Dathan and Abiram are refusing to even come and speak with him, as if he does not have enough on his plate. My frustration level would have been off the charts at this point! But Moses does not take his frustration out on the unlucky messenger delivering the Reubenites' response. Instead, he rightly brings his concerns to God.

Moses has come a long way from the arrogant, impulsive man of his youth. Remember his reaction when he saw an Egyptian mistreating an Israelite? After looking around to make sure there were not any witnesses, Moses killed the man! The next day, he stepped into the middle of a fight between two Israelites. He questioned the man he felt was in the wrong and learned that his involvement in the previous day's murder was known. Moses fled. Arriving in Midian, he drove away the shepherds who were harassing a group of female shepherds (Exodus 2:11–22).

Forty years of tending sheep in the desert has changed Moses. He no longer takes matters into his own hands. Instead, he pours his heart out to God. How do you respond to frustrations and difficulties? Do you kill the messenger, venting your irritation with whomever happens to be around? Unfortunately, for many of us, that seems to be our go-to response. But God instructs us to "be quick to hear, slow to speak, slow to anger; for the anger of man does not produce the righteousness of God" (James 1:19–20). Here, Moses is a good example of someone who is responding in a godly way.

It is important to note that there should not be a third party involved in our disputes. If we have a problem with someone, we need to speak directly to that person. This is one instance where Korah actually got it right. His complaint was with Moses and Aaron, and he spoke directly to them. However, we are instructed to speak to God first. Korah's actions reveal this is something he did not do.

"And Moses was very angry and said to the LORD, 'Do not respect their offering. I have not taken one donkey from them, and I have not harmed one of them'" (Numbers 16:15).

We learn four things from Moses' statement (another list!). First, we are told that he is angry. But not just angry. Very angry! In fact, this is the *only* time we are told Moses was very angry. The Hebrew word for very in this verse is *mod* (pronounced "mode"). The only other time *mod* refers to Moses' anger is when he came down from Mount Sinai to find the Israelites worshipping the golden calf. Usually *mod* is used to describe God's wrath.[54] This suggests Moses' anger was a righteous anger. He is outraged by the things that outrage God.

Next, Moses makes a request. He asks God to reject the Reubenites' offering. What offering is Moses referring to? When we have a question, we should first look to the context for answers.

When we have a question, we should first look to the context for answers.

Reading the verses surrounding this statement leads us to understand that Moses is probably speaking of the incense offering. This offering is to take place the following day. While we have taken our time looking at background information for this rebellion, we must remember everything we have discussed so far regarding this event has occurred on the same day.

People have been making offerings and sacrifices to God for almost as long as the human race has existed. In the beginning, Adam and Eve could approach God directly. This was the ideal, but it did not last long. Soon they sinned, doing something God told them not to do. They ate the fruit God forbade them to eat. When God came to them afterward, their instinct was to hide from Him. The first sacrifice occurred after Adam and Eve's sin. God took the life of an animal and used the skin to clothe Adam and Eve. The animal paid the price for Adam and Eve's sin (Genesis 3).

In Genesis chapter 4 we find Cain and Abel, the sons of Adam and Eve, each bringing an offering to God. Offerings such as these allowed people to approach God indirectly. These sacrifices were necessary from the time sin entered the world up until Jesus died on the cross and rose from the dead, paying the penalty for all of our sins. In this early instance, Abel's offering was accepted but Cain's was not. So when Moses asked God to reject the Reubenites' offering, he was asking God to treat them as He treated Cain. Moses was asking God to deny Dathan and Abiram access to Him. At that time it was not unusual for an offering from a disrespectful person to be refused.[55]

Moses then states that he has not taken anything from these Reubenites, not even a donkey. Which raises the question: What does a donkey have to do with anything? To gain some insight, we need to follow the cross-reference. In this case it directs us to a future leader of Israel, the prophet Samuel.

Just as God is leading the Israelites in the desert, He continues to lead their nation once they reach the Promised Land. In the desert, God speaks through Moses. In the Promised Land, God speaks through the judges and the prophets. But the Israelites were not happy with this arrangement. Instead, they wanted to have a king, just like the nations surrounding them (1 Samuel 8:5).

God tells Samuel the downside of Israel having an earthly king. As a prophet, it is Samuel's job to relay this message to the people. One of God's warnings about an earthly king is that "he will take your male servants and female servants and the best of your young men and your donkeys, and put them to his work" (1 Samuel 8:16). Later, Samuel says to the people, "Witness against me before the LORD and before His anointed: Whose ox have I taken, or whose donkey have I taken, or whom have I cheated?" (1 Samuel 12:3 NIV).

Samuel, like Moses before him, is saying that he has not elevated himself over the people or taken advantage of them. In other words, he has not acted like a king over them. Neither of them has benefitted from leadership in any tangible way.

Finally, Moses says he has not harmed anyone. Other Bible translations say he has not wronged anyone (NIV) or has not mistreated (HCSB) even one of them. The Egyptian Moses might have taken matters into his own hands and eliminated the problem. But this desert-taught Moses promptly goes to God, pours out his grievances, and leaves them there. Moses has learned not to take these rebellious actions personally. He knows God will handle them.

Digging Deeper

What do the following verses have to say about our words?

Proverbs 10:19 When words are many, Trangression is not lacking, but whoever restrains their lips is prudent.

Proverbs 17:27 Whoever restrains his words has knowledge, and he who has a cool spirit is a man of understanding

Ecclesiastes 5:2

Do not be quick with your mouth, do not be hasty in your heart to utter anything before God.

Self-Discovery

How do you respond to frustrations and difficulties?

Short

Has this changed over time? If so, in what way?

We are all a leader in some form, whether at home, at work or in ministry. As a leader how can you exercise patience?

How can you avoid exasperating a leader if you are the one being led? prayer and support.

Chapter 15

The Instructions

Moses lets out a deep sigh. Before he calls it a day, he must speak to Korah. One. More. Time. Moses gives instructions similar to those he gave at the onset of this rebellion. "Be present, you and all your company, before the LORD, you and they, and Aaron, tomorrow. And let every one of you take his censer and put incense on it, and every one of you bring before the LORD his censer, 250 censers; you also, and Aaron, each his censer" (Numbers 16:16–17).

As we learned previously, repetition emphasizes what is being said. These instructions, given twice, should set off alarm bells. Korah, however, does not give any indication of being worried. But Moses knows there is reason for alarm.

Everyone should know.

After all, lives have already been lost.

God chose Aaron and his four sons, Nadab, Abihu, Eleazar, and Ithamar, to serve Him as priests. The five priests were all ordained in Leviticus chapters eight and nine, a process that lasted eight days. Then, "Nadab and Abihu, the sons of Aaron, each took his censer and put fire in it and laid incense on it and offered unauthorized fire before the LORD, which he had not commanded them. And fire came out from before the LORD and consumed them, and they died before the LORD" (Leviticus 10:1–2).

How could Korah and his men be unconcerned about something as serious as this? This event is so important, it is mentioned in Scripture another four times! "The Hebrew phrase for what Nadab and Abihu offered is *esh zarah*. The word *esh* means fire, and *zarah* (translated above as unauthorized) is an adjective identifying something as strange, foreign, or illegitimate."[56] The NASB dictionary translates *zarah* as a loathsome thing.

Nadab and Abihu offered something that was not consecrated or holy. Something that God did not accept. They paid for this error with their lives. And they were priests! Perhaps this is why the Reubenites refused to come to Moses. They may have recalled this event and decided it would be safer to keep their distance from Korah. After all, their beef was with Moses, not Aaron.

Asking questions is a key to understanding the Bible.

Asking questions is a key to understanding the Bible. Two of the questions I have about this passage are, "What is a censer?" and "If priests are the ones responsible for offering incense, and now there are only three priests, where did the 250 censers come from?"

Did you notice the emphasis on censers in the verses at the beginning of this chapter? They are mentioned four times in just one verse! A censer, also known as a fire pan, was a vessel used to transport hot coals. As part of the altar, the censers Nadab and Abihu used were holy. Because of this, only fire taken from the altar, which was also holy, would be acceptable.[57] Nadab and Abihu offered unholy fire and in an instant were dead. Instead of five priests, there were now only three.

While I could find no definitive answer on where the 250 censers came from, there are several theories:

- Every home had a censer for household use.[58] It could be used to transport burning embers from the fire to a stove or to borrow hot coals from a neighbor if their own fire had been extinguished.
- Ornate firepans came from Egypt as part of the plunder.[59]
- Each family brought a censer they previously used to worship household gods back in Egypt. (This would be especially offensive to God.)
- These men did not have their own censors. They each either made one quickly or used another vessel for that purpose.

There is also the question of the incense Korah and his followers would offer. God gave artisans a specific recipe for incense; the *only* incense God would accept. Consisting of sweet spices and frankincense, this compound was only to be used by priests when serving in the tabernacle. It is doubtful Korah had access to this recipe. Even if he did, he was forbidden to make it.

Was Korah so intent on being a priest that he neglected all of God's warnings? We can be so fixated on what we want that we totally miss what God is actually telling us. When my husband first suggested we go on a mission trip to Kenya, I thought he had lost his mind! Because of chronic pain, I could not keep up with even the basics of everyday life. I was not sure how I would manage the trip half-way around the planet, let alone function once we arrived.

Then it occurred to me that I could just go to the informational meeting with my husband. Once there, I would be honest about my limitations. No one in their right mind would want someone like me along on their trip. I was confident that they, as Christians, would be kind as they totally rejected me. My husband would be pleased, I wouldn't have to go, and we would all live happily ever after.

Except they didn't reject me! I thought, "What is the matter with these people? Have they no standards?" From then on, I prayed fervently, "Please God, make it clear that this is *not* what you want me to do!" (As a new Christian, I did not understand it is not a good idea to tell God what to do.)

Every time I felt Him speak to me through a verse in Scripture, I wrote it down. I wrestled with God for months before I finally got the message, spoken to a fellow coward, Gideon. "Go in the strength you have. . . . Am I not sending you?" (Judges 6:14 NIV). How could I argue with that? I'm surprised my picture didn't show up next to those words, they were so specific to my situation.

> Are you so focused on what you want (or don't want) that you fail to listen to God's plan?

Funny thing though. Long after the trip, I returned to the list of verses God gave to me:

- I am with you (Genesis 28:15).
- I will go before you (Deuteronomy 31:8).
- I will watch over you (Genesis 28:15 NIV).
- I will not let your foot slip (Psalm 121:3 NIV).
- I will not in any way fail you (Hebrews 13:5).[60]

God was telling me all along that I should travel to Kenya! But I was so focused on looking for the "no," I almost missed the "go." Are you so focused on what you want (or don't want) that you fail to listen to God's plan?

I wonder if something similar happened with Korah. Was he so focused on looking for "Yes, you can be a priest" that he missed all of God's "no's"?

- No, you are not a descendant of Aaron. You cannot be a priest.
- No, you do not have access to holy fire. You cannot be a priest.
- No, you do not have the proper incense. You do not have the recipe. You are not even allowed to make that incense. You cannot be a priest.

This offering will take place the following day. This gives Korah and his followers time to think about what they are planning to do. Did Korah stop to think that he is not supposed to offer incense to God? That God would not accept just any incense or any fire? If priests died for making an offering incorrectly, what did Korah think would happen to him?

Moses is not setting up a trap for Korah and his cohorts. Moses gave these instructions twice. In each instance, Moses spoke to God immediately beforehand. These instructions did not come from Moses. These instructions came from God.

God gives Korah and his followers the opportunity to change their minds. Unfortunately, we are not told that anyone chose to do so. Only God knows what made Korah and his cohorts think they could do something that even Aaron's sons could not do and live to tell about it. It appears history will repeat itself. In this case, this is a bad thing.

A very bad thing.

Digging Deeper

List reasons why it is important to obey God.

Romans 8:28

Self-Discovery

Read Psalm 121, but first pray and ask God to speak to you. Record what you feel God is saying to you.

That I can ~~to~~ depend on him in every respect of my life. He does not slumber ~~[illegible]~~ or sleep. He is always on duty.

2/7/24

Prayer Request

1 Justin - brooken clavol

2 KAYA - Heart surgory body be able to adjust when ventilator is taken out. He is 11 Ruth's niece ? is Justin mom

Dave's Afib stopped today

3 Charlotte

4 CORA

PART FOUR

The Reckoning

(Numbers 16:18–40)

Chapter 16

The Congregation

Moses and Aaron exit their tents and stand solemnly before the tabernacle.[61] As the sun peeks over the horizon behind them, people begin to gather. The sun, with its scorching heat, is the one constant in the desert. Perhaps that is why some people began to worship it. The Egyptians named their sun god Ra and credited him with creating the universe as well as all of their other gods.[62]

Every time the Israelites relocate, the Levites faithfully erect the tabernacle in the center of camp. Its entrance always faces east as God commands. After Adam and Eve committed the first sin, God banished them from the Garden of Eden and sent them east. To keep them away from the tree of life, He stationed an angel with a flaming sword at the east end of the garden. Since this time, traveling west symbolizes moving toward God while going east represents moving away from Him.[63]

With the tabernacle courtyard's entrance to the east, those who enter are moving west, toward God's presence. This positioning forces former worshippers of Ra to turn their backs on the sun god as they move toward the one true God.

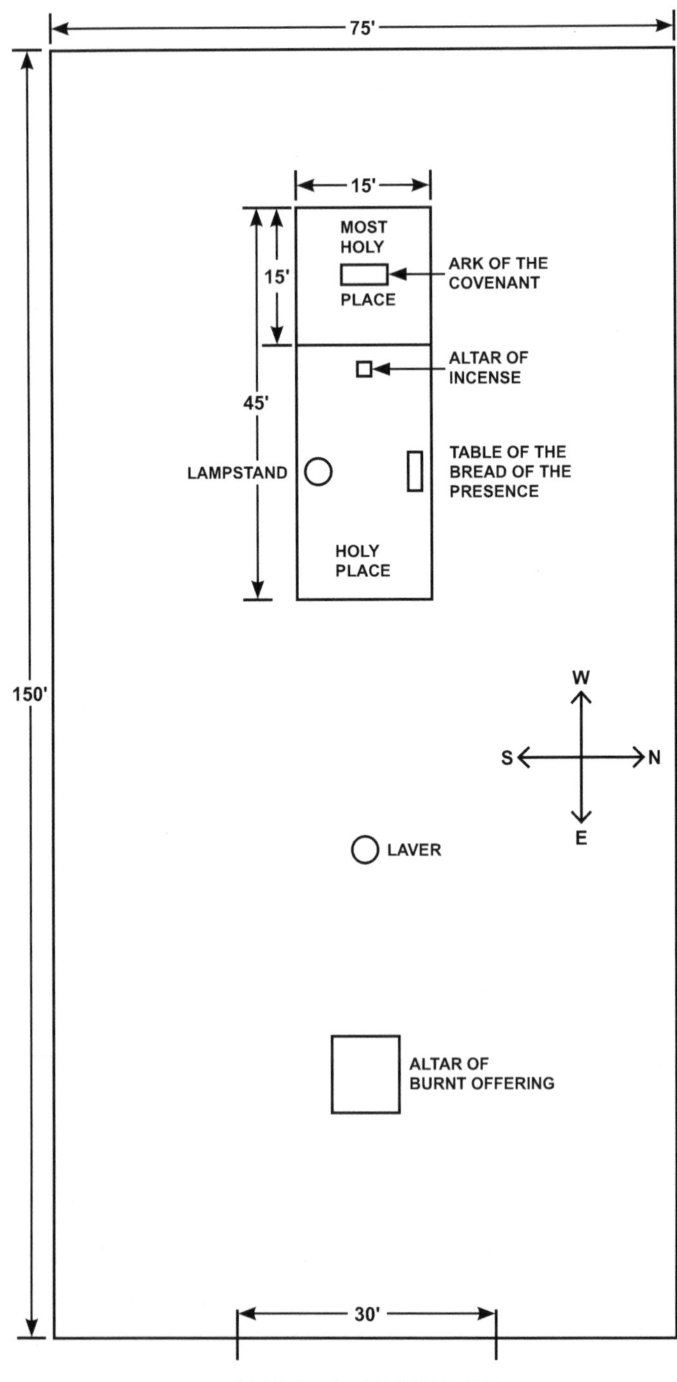

PLAN OF THE TABERNACLE

The tabernacle proper is a relatively small covered structure located near the west end of the courtyard. It measures forty-five feet long, fifteen feet wide and fifteen feet tall.[64] *Only the priests* are allowed to pass through the entrance to the first room, known as the Holy Place. It contains three objects, each made according to God's specifications.

To the left is a seven-branched lampstand (*menorah*) made of pure gold. Aaron, the high priest, tends to the lamps both in the morning and in the evening. This lampstand burns olive oil and provides light, both in the Holy Place and the Most Holy Place.

To the right is the table of showbread. Every week the Levites make twelve loaves of bread, placing frankincense on it to keep it fresh. On the Sabbath, the high priest places the fresh bread on the table. The previous week's bread is removed and eaten by the priests "in a holy place" (Leviticus 24:5–9). This was still being performed about 400 years later when David and his men ate the showbread as they fled from King Saul (1 Samuel 21:1–6).

Just in front of the curtain separating the Holy Place from the Most Holy Place is the altar of incense. This altar is just eighteen inches square and three feet tall, with a horn on top of each corner. Here God's exclusive blend of incense is continually burned. Beyond the curtain lies the Most Holy Place, also known as the Holy of Holies. It contains just one item, the ark of the covenant. The high priest alone is allowed to enter this most sacred place and then only once a year, on the Day of Atonement.

Many of the cities the Israelites passed on their journey were surrounded by a wall for protection. The city gate served multiple purposes beyond allowing people in or keeping them out. Abraham went to the city gate of Hebron to purchase a burial place for his wife Sarah. Elders gathered at the gate to settle disputes and judge cases. Punishments were sometimes given there.

Similarly, the tabernacle proper is surrounded by a wall of curtains seven and a half feet tall. This wall prevents any person or animal from accidentally going where they are not allowed. The tabernacle proper is twice as tall as the wall, so it can be seen above the surrounding curtains. The entrance, on the east end, is also known as the gate. It is here that God will make His decision and mete out justice to the rebels.

Moses ended the previous day by relaying God's instructions to Aaron, Korah, and the 250 community leaders. Now "every man took his censer and put fire in them and laid incense on them and stood at the entrance of the tent of meeting with Moses and Aaron. Then Korah assembled all the congregation against them at the entrance of the tent of meeting. And the glory of the LORD appeared to all the congregation" (Numbers 16:18–19).

It appears as though Moses and Aaron were first joined by the 250 leaders, followed by the congregation. The congregation refers to *everyone* in camp. Now, this multitude did not merely wander to the gate of the tabernacle on their own. Look again at Numbers 16:19. Korah rounded them up! Is Korah that confident God will choose him to be the new high priest? Has he gathered everyone to be witnesses to his anticipated shining moment?

This verse tells us Korah gathered the Israelites "against them." My friend Mary is not a fan of pronouns. I can hear her asking, "Who is 'them' referring to?" Sometimes looking in different translations can help clarify a reference. In this case, I did not find this verse worded differently, but I did find a cross-reference in the NIV translation.

Looking in different translations can help clarify a reference.

In both Numbers 16:42 and 20:2 we are told they gathered in opposition to Moses and Aaron. So, this is clearly yet another attack on God's chosen leaders.

What is Korah thinking?

Maybe he isn't.

Not only does Korah want the top spot, he also wants Moses and Aaron put in their place. That is, according to Korah, beneath him. He should know by now that God has placed Moses and Aaron at the top of the chain of command, and that is where they will stay.

Korah wants to be a priest so much that he can taste it. He must know he does not meet God's requirements, yet he continues to insist he should be included in the priesthood. He is beyond confident; he is arrogant! This reminds me of another arrogant man, Pharaoh. Scripture tells us God hardened Pharaoh's heart. But when we look at that event in context, we discover Pharaoh hardened his own heart multiple times before God hardened it. Perhaps God told Korah and his followers to offer incense because that is the only thing that will get through to Korah and his own hardened heart. But by then, it will be too late.

Numbers 16:19 also reveals that all the people gathered there saw the glory of the Lord. God appears as a cloud by day and a pillar of fire by night as the Israelites follow Him through the desert. But the glory of the Lord is something more. Can you even imagine what God's glory looks like? I have a hard time picturing this, but the Bible does give us a few hints.

When the people rebelled in the wilderness of Sin, "the glory of the Lord appeared in the cloud" (Exodus 16:10). So, God's glory is something distinct from the cloud that leads the Israelites. At the time the Ten Commandments were given, we are told "the appearance of the glory of the LORD was like a devouring fire" (Exodus 24:17). The glory of the Lord is something the Israelites have seen before, but only on certain occasions. Do you think they realize how much God has blessed them by allowing them to see His glory?

Digging Deeper

Read the following verses and record who is moving and in which direction they're moving:

Genesis 4:16

Genesis 13:11

Genesis 25:5–6

Numbers 34:14–15

Read Ezekiel 1:28. What do you learn about the Glory of the Lord?

Self-Discovery

Describe a time when you were moving away from God. Did you do this knowingly, or did you only realize this after the fact?

Chapter 17

The Pardon

When Moses first heard of Korah's rebellion, he immediately laid on his face before God.

Praying.

And listening.

Then he stood up and explained how God would identify the people He considered to be holy. In Numbers 16:15 Moses spoke to God again, then Moses reported to Korah what would be expected from him today. So far in this account of Korah's rebellion, we have heard God's messages only through Moses. For the first time in this account, we now hear from God directly: "The Lord spoke to Moses and to Aaron, saying, 'Separate yourselves from among this congregation, that I may consume them in a moment.' And they fell on their faces and said, 'O God, the God of the spirits of all flesh, shall one man sin, and will you be angry with all the congregation?'" (Numbers 16:20–22).

Would you believe this statement is even harsher than it sounds? The Hebrew word *kalah,* translated consume, means to annihilate, destroy utterly or to obliterate.[65] Yikes! God says that

He will destroy the rebels in a moment. When I hear that phrase, I think of a short period of time. Like when a store clerk is busy helping someone else and they tell you they will be with you "in a moment." But that is not what this Hebrew word, *rega,* means. The NIV translates it as "at once," and the HCSB as "instantly."

In the previous chapter we determined the congregation is made up of *every single member* of this group traveling through the desert. So, it is as if God is saying, "Step aside Moses and Aaron, while I instantly kill off everyone else!" This makes me wonder. If God has the power to wipe out all of these people, and of course He does, why does God first tell Moses and Aaron his plan? Why doesn't He just obliterate all but the two of them?

The answer is found in the cross-reference. Following the cross-reference gives us insight into a passage. This directs us to Genesis 18, where God does something similar. God tells Abraham His plan to obliterate Sodom and Gomorrah. Why does God make His intentions known? Let's look at a couple of reasons.

Following the cross-references gives us insight into a passage.

First, God is announcing what will happen *if no one intercedes.* The fact that He verbalizes this message is actually a prompt for the recipient to speak up.[66] God is giving Moses and Aaron the opportunity to plead with Him on behalf of His people. God allows Himself to be persuaded, and lives are spared. In Abraham's case, just a handful of lives; for Moses and Aaron, thousands. In each case, someone pleaded to God, and God altered His plans. This is great news, my friends!

Notice how quickly Moses and Aaron were on their faces before God, pleading for the lives of the congregation. They were well aware that God meant to wipe out everyone that instant. But they did not even take a minute to think things over. Unlike Abraham before them, they did not begin negotiating with God. Even though life would undoubtably be easier without the troublemakers, they prayed for everyone. Or maybe everyone except one. I find that to be remarkable. After all, how quickly do you stop to pray for someone who is causing you problems? Unfortunately, I know that is rarely my first response.

> We begin to recognize God at work in our own lives when we learn how He has worked in the past.

Events like these demonstrate the power of prayer. This should be an encouragement to us all! God is the same yesterday, today, and forever. We begin to recognize God at work in our own lives when we learn how He has worked in the past. God changed course after hearing the pleas of Abraham, Moses, and Aaron. This means He is capable of doing the same for us as we come to Him in prayer!

Second, announcing the outcome makes it clear that the result is from God. This gives Him the credit, making it impossible to declare the aftermath happened by chance. My husband likened this to someone calling a shot during a game of pool. If a cue stick I held directed a ball into a pocket, that would be dumb luck. But if a skilled player called a shot before he made it, when the ball went into the pocket everyone would know it did not just happen by accident. The player knew exactly what he was going to do before he did it.

The same is true for God. Since He told Abraham what He was going to do beforehand, it was clear that Sodom and Gomorrah were not destroyed because of a natural disaster. God purposely destroyed these cities because of the unrepentant sin of their residents.

This was not a coincidence; this was a consequence.

In his plea found in verse 22 above, Moses refers to God as "the God of the spirits of all flesh." This is a unique name for God. This name is used again only once, in Numbers 27:16. In that instance, Moses asks God to choose a leader who will shepherd the people as they enter the Promised Land. This name means God knows a person's heart, their inner motives.[67]

God may seem harsh for wanting to wipe out the entire community, but we must remember these people are not blameless. With the exception of Joshua and Caleb, every single person twenty years of age or older is already sentenced to death in the desert for refusing to enter the Promised Land.

Are you familiar with the phrase, "To whom much is given, of him much will be required"? Hopefully you are, since Jesus is the one who said it (Luke 12:48)! Think of all that God had given to this group of people:

- God gave them their *freedom*. Their parents did not know what freedom felt like, but now they were free.
- God *provided* for them by moving the Egyptians to give them plunder as they left Egypt.
- God *protected* them from the advancing Egyptian army.
- God *supplied* this multitude with the nourishment they needed every day.
- God *led* them to the Promised Land. The only reason they were not there already was because they refused to enter.
- God allowed the entire congregation to *see His glory* on several occasions.

Most of the members in this congregation were formerly slaves. They basically had no say in anything. Their only option was to obey their oppressors or face the consequences. Suddenly they are given their freedom and they do not know how to handle it. It is as if they have been beaten down for so long that their only instinct is to rebel, just because they can. Despite all God has done for them, when Korah announces his showdown with Moses and Aaron, every member of the congregation comes running.

Finally, in their plea, Moses and Aaron ask God if the entire community should be punished because of one man's sin. That one man is Korah. Notice the different factions involved here:

Korah influenced his neighbors, the Reubenites Dathan and Abiram.

Korah indirectly recruited 250 leaders to join in the rebellion.

Korah rounded up the entire community.

The common denominator here is Korah. He is the source of all of this rebellion. Judgment is coming, but in his arrogance, Korah does not see it.

Digging Deeper

What do you learn about falling on your face from the following passages?

Joshua 5:14

2 Samuel 14:4

Daniel 8:17

Self-Discovery

How quickly do you stop to pray for someone who is causing you problems?

Share a time when you felt God acted on your behalf.

Chapter 18

The Warning

I believe bus drivers are unsung heroes. They have a difficult job, especially those who transport children to and from school. With such precious cargo, the driver has his or her work cut out for them. This is especially true when they are the only adult on board. Being a mom, I can really relate to this. Let's face it, transporting children can be difficult when you have to be both chauffeur and referee.

Imagine you are the bus driver. All sixty-five seats are filled with excited students embarking on a long trip. You do not make it far before you hear a disturbance. It gets louder and louder until it reaches the point where you need to pull the bus over to the side of the road. You walk down the aisle to discover what the problem is. You must restore order before things get out of hand.

You return to your seat and resume your journey, but it is not long before another disturbance arises. After that one is settled, there is another. And another. And another. Imagine your frustration level! You are never going to make it to your destination if you must keep stopping the bus to do crowd control.

Welcome to Moses' world.

But Moses is not leading sixty-five students. He is just one man leading hundreds of thousands of people, minimum! God has made it very clear that Moses is His chosen leader, and that only Aaron and his descendants can be priests. This is the eleventh rebellion Moses has to deal with, and these people still have about thirty-eight more years to travel together in the desert. If they are ever going to reach the Promised Land, it is vital that they get their act together. This is one reason why God's consequences are so severe.

"The LORD spoke to Moses, saying, 'Say to the congregation, Get away from the dwelling of Korah, Dathan, and Abiram.' Then Moses rose and went to Dathan and Abiram, and the elders of Israel followed him" (Numbers 16:23–25).

The previous day, Dathan and Abiram refused to come when Moses sent for them. Instead, they chose to air their complaints to the messenger. Now, it is Moses who goes to them, and he does not need to travel far. He just walked around the corner to his left, to the south side of the tabernacle.

If you remember our camping diagram in *Enough* chapter five, the Kohathites, including Korah, camped between the tabernacle and the tribe of Reuben. Korah must have set up his tent on the southern end of the Kohathite clan, while Dathan and Abiram camped on the northern end of the Reubenites. The three families appear to be camping back-to-back, since God sends Moses to just one place.

All the better to grumble together, I assume.

In answer to Moses and Aaron's prayer in Numbers 16:22, God will spare the congregation. This is no small thing. According to the law, anyone who disobeys God's chosen leader deserves to be put to death. But here, in the midst of an all-out rebellion, we see God's grace. It can be easy to forget this with the upcoming tragedy.

"God's grace initially may feel hot and raw, like the aftermath of a sunburn, before it soothes and heals."[68]

Moses warns the congregation to move away from the ringleaders of the rebellion, so no one else is caught in the upcoming judgment. "And he spoke to the congregation, saying, 'Depart, please, from the tents of these wicked men, and touch nothing of theirs, lest you be swept away with all their sins'" (Numbers 16:26).

"Be swept away" is a translation of the Hebrew word *saphah.*[69] This same word is used twice in the warning the angels gave to Lot and his family as they escaped from Sodom. The King James Version of the Bible translates *saphah* as both "consumed," and "destroyed." Thankfully, the congregation heeded Moses' warning.

Because God is holy, He cannot tolerate anything unclean in the camp. These rebels are considered to be unclean because of their sin of rebellion. As a result, everything they touch is unclean. That is why the congregation is warned not to touch anything belonging to these three rebels. If anyone does so, they will be destroyed as well.

> So they got away from the dwelling of Korah, Dathan, and Abiram. And Dathan and Abiram came out and stood at the door of their tents, together with their wives, their sons, and their little ones. And Moses said, "Hereby you shall know that the Lord has sent me to do all these works, and that it has not been of my own accord. If these men die as all men die, or if they are visited by the fate of all mankind, then the Lord has not sent me. But if the Lord creates something new, and the ground opens its mouth and swallows them up with all that belongs to them, and they go down alive into Sheol, then you shall know that these men have despised the Lord." (Numbers 16:27–30)

Here we see God calling His shot. He is telling the people exactly what will happen before it takes place. This clarifies that what comes next is a consequence, not a coincidence. God is making it abundantly clear that rebels will not be tolerated.

Connectives (formerly known as conjunctions) are parts of speech that link up "words and phrases and clauses."[70] *But* is the connective I find to be the most helpful in my studies. The word *but* always signals a contrast. When we see it, we should compare what is before the word *but* with what comes afterwards.

The word **but** always signals a contrast.

Here, God mentions ordinary death before the *but*. After it, God specifies that the earth will open up and the rebels and all that belongs to them will fall in. God could have the men die on the spot, but instead He says He is going to create something new. The word translated "create" is the Hebrew word *bara*. Literally translated, this word means to "create a creation."[71] In the Old Testament, *bara* is used only in reference to "God's divine activity."[72] *Bara* is also found in the very first verse of the Bible: "In the beginning, God *bara* the heavens and the earth" (Genesis 1:1). In both instances, God made or did something that had not been done before.

Some scholars suggest the tents of Korah, Dathan, and Abiram were built on a *kewir*. That is a bog with a hard crust of dried mud on top of it. If this hard surface breaks, everything on it would fall into the mud.[73] But that would not be something new, unless this was the first time one appeared. I wonder if God is referring to the world's first earthquake . . .

Can you imagine how terrifying it would be to witness
the earth splitting open right before you?
Or worse yet, beneath you?

Digging Deeper

Read Deuteronomy 17:12–13 in several different translations. How are the person's actions described?

Do you think this accurately describes Korah and his associates? Why or why not.

Why do you think God requires the death penalty in these situations?

Self-Discovery

Have you ever witnessed something traumatic? If so, how did it change you?

Chapter 19

The Disappearance

My husband and I are on a rare date night downtown. Strolling along the river, enjoying the sound of rushing water, I stop to tie my shoe. Bob continues walking, now ahead of me. Suddenly, I hear shouting. As I walk closer, I realize the man screaming is accusing Bob of punching him! What am I going to do? Do I turn around and pretend I do not know Bob? Should I call the police? What does one do in a situation like this?

Have you ever found yourself in a position where you do not know what to do or how to think? I find myself in such a place reading these next verses. Moses barely finished relaying God's message to Dathan and Abiram when

> The ground under them split apart. And the earth opened its mouth and swallowed them up, with their households and all the people who belonged to Korah and all their goods. So they and all that belonged to them went down alive into Sheol, and the earth closed over them, and they perished from the midst of the assembly. And all Israel who were around them fled at

> their cry, for they said, "Lest the earth swallow us up!" And fire came out from the LORD and consumed the 250 men offering the incense. (Numbers 16:31–35)

Confusion.

Panic.

Tragedy.

Can we start by stating the obvious? This is a very difficult passage. In situations like this, it is helpful to remember that understanding God is like trying to pour a million gallons of information into a one-quart head.[74] There are things that are just beyond our limited ability to comprehend.

In Numbers 16:12, Dathan and Abiram refused to come *up* to see Moses. Here we see a contrast, for now they will go *down*, under the surface of the earth, into Sheol. So what exactly is Sheol? At that time, people held these beliefs:

- Sheol was "a place of separation from God.
- "A shadowy place of no return."[75]
- "The dwelling place of the dead, both the wicked and the good.
- "A place of watery silence and darkness from which there is no escape."[76]

At that time, Sheol was believed to be a place where everyone went after death. People did not believe there was a separation between good and evil in the afterlife. For example, After Jacob was told (untruthfully) that his son Joseph was dead, he replied, "I shall go down to Sheol to my son, mourning" (Genesis 37:35).

In 1 Samuel 28, King Saul became fearful when the Philistine army gathered nearby. When God did not answer Saul's pleas according to his own timetable, he sent for a medium (something

God forbids). He asked her to bring up the prophet Samuel, whom he believed was underground in Sheol. These are two examples of good people presumed to be in Sheol.

In contrast, after the Israelites were freed from Babylon, Isaiah 14 records a song of contempt they will sing against their former captors. It says, in part, that Sheol is eager to welcome Israel's enemies. The defeated kings there will taunt Babylon. The ones who thought they would rise up into the heavens will instead sink into the deepest part of Sheol.

There is another contrast between the information about Sheol I just shared and what Numbers 16:31–35 says. Sheol is a place for the dead, but Numbers 16:33 tells us that those who went down there were still alive! The fact that they were still living when they went to Sheol is thought to indicate that these people, being conscious, would suffer more intensely than those who went there in the normal fashion, after death.[77]

The three events listed in Numbers 16:31–35 appear to happen quickly, one after the other. First, the earth opens and the rebels, their families, and all their possessions fall in. The ground then closes up over them. Next, everyone nearby runs away, afraid they too would be swallowed up. Finally, the 250 leaders are devoured by fire sent from God.

Why did the people fear they would be swallowed up like the Reubenites? Looking back at the context can help answer *why* questions.

Looking back at the context can help answer **why** questions.

In Numbers 16:21, God told Moses and Aaron He was going to destroy the *entire* congregation. That is because, just a few verses before that, Korah gathered up everyone to come against Moses and Aaron. This entire community was going to be wiped out because they were guilty of siding with Korah. They could have chosen to stay in their tents, but instead they came to stand against God's chosen leaders.

The only reason the entire group was not killed at that time was because Moses and Aaron prayed God would spare the group from judgment. So the congregation may have feared for their lives and run away because they knew they were guilty. Evidently, they did not know God well enough to know His character. They still did not understand that God does not go back on His word.

It is understandable that the rebels were punished for their actions. After all, they were warned against rebelling many times. The difficulty comes with the knowledge that Dathan's and Abiram's "wives, their sons, and their little ones" (Numbers 16:27) were also swallowed up into the earth.

The story at the beginning of this chapter is an illustration, not a factual account. My husband Bob is the kindest, most patient, loving, soft-spoken person I have ever met. To my knowledge he has never punched anyone. He rarely raises his voice. Even when I accidently backed into our *brand-new* garage door, he said nothing (although I could tell he was using a *lot* of restraint.)

If that were a true story, I would not turn and walk away. Nor would I call the police. Why? Because, after thirty years of marriage, I know Bob. I know his character. I know there would either be some mistake, something I did not know, or something extremely serious that happened to give Bob a reason to act in that way.[78]

> When we do not understand God's actions, we must remember His character.

Even more so, this is true of God.

When we do not understand God's actions, we must remember His character.

It is important to remember God is all-knowing. He knows our hearts. "You know everything I do; from far away you understand all my thoughts" (Psalm 139:2 GNT). God knows our actions, and He knows our motives. God knows who is good and who is evil.

God is righteous; He always does the right thing. "The Lord is your mighty defender, perfect and just in all his ways; Your God is faithful and true; he does what is right and fair" (Deuteronomy 32:4 GNT).

God always acts with our best interests in mind. "Come and see what our God has done, what awesome miracles he performs for people!" (Psalm 66:5 NLT).

"For my thoughts are not your thoughts, neither are your ways my ways, declares the Lord. For as the heavens are higher than the earth, so are my ways higher than your ways and my thoughts than your thoughts" (Isaiah 55:8–9).

There are times when we will leave God's Word with unanswered questions, and that is okay.

Digging Deeper

Read Leviticus 19:31 and Deuteronomy 18:9–14. What does God have to say about consulting mediums?

Record what you learn about God's character from each of these passages:

Job 34:10–11

Psalm 51:4

Jeremiah 30:11

Self-Discovery

What is God calling us to do in each of these passages? Which is the most challenging for you?

Philippians 2:14

James 1:19–21

1 John 1:8–10

Chapter 20

Eleazar

Korah and his fellow rebels receive judgment from God Himself. This should not come as a surprise to any of them. The men who want Moses' job—earthly power—go down alive into the earth. Those who want Aaron's job—spiritual power—receive an F (as in fire) and "go up as a burnt offering to heaven."[79]

As harsh as it seems to us, this was for the good of the community. One scholar likened it to "shooting a suicide attacker before he managed to detonate his bomb."[80] It does not appear the rest of the congregation saw it this way, because they all ran away in fear. Immediately after the 250 community leaders were reduced to ashes, God spoke to Moses and said,

> "Tell Eleazar son of Aaron, the priest, to remove the censers from the charred remains and scatter the coals some distance away, for the censers are holy—the censers of the men who sinned at the cost of their lives. Hammer the censers into sheets to overlay the altar, for they were presented before the LORD and have become holy. Let them be a sign to the Israelites." So Eleazar

> the priest collected the bronze censers brought by those who had been burned to death, and he had them hammered out to overlay the altar, as the LORD directed him through Moses. (Numbers 16:37–40 NIV)

This may be the worst day of Eleazar's life. Or perhaps his worst day was when his brothers Nadab and Abihu died when offering unauthorized fire to the LORD. Can you imagine how traumatic it must have been for Eleazar, seeing scores of men killed in the same way his brothers died? Now picture yourself having to do his job!

God instructs Eleazar to dig through the 250 cremated bodies to retrieve the bronze censers, which are now holy. Then he has to dispose of what is left of the 250 rebels outside of the camp. This gruesome task was not given to Aaron, because any contact with the dead makes a person ceremonially unclean. Aaron must remain clean so he can offer the incense to God twice daily. The now-holy censers can be used only in God's service and can be handled only by a priest. They could not again be used for ordinary purposes.[81]

In *Enough* chapter 16 we looked at a diagram of the tabernacle. Our focus then was on the tabernacle proper, which contains the Holy Place and the Most Holy Place. The tabernacle proper is at the west end of a large courtyard. The courtyard is the only place that an ordinary Israelite is allowed to enter. The first thing a man would see after passing through the surrounding curtain is the altar of burnt offering.

A craftsman named "Bezalel constructed the altar of burnt offering from acacia wood. It was square, 7½ feet long and 7½ feet wide, and was 4½ feet high. He made horns for it on its four corners; the horns were of one piece. Then he overlaid it with bronze" (Exodus 38:1–2 HCSB). This altar is also known as the bronze altar. It features a grate for the animal sacrifices that are burned. There is also a ring on each corner of the altar. These hold the poles the Kohathites use to carry it when it is time to move the tabernacle.

When a man needed to make a sin offering, he brought with him a sheep or goat without any flaws. Laying his hand on the animal's head, he would confess his sins. This symbolized sin leaving him and moving onto the animal. He then had to kill this animal himself, giving the animal the penalty he himself deserved. "And the priest shall take some of its blood with his finger and put it on the horns of the altar of burnt offering and pour out all the rest of its blood at the base of the altar" (Leviticus 4:30).

This is the altar that Eleazar is to cover with the flattened bronze censers. "This was to remind the Israelites that no one except a descendant of Aaron should come to burn incense before the LORD, or he would become like Korah and his followers" (Numbers 16:40 NIV). Now the Israelites had a visual reminder of this rebellion every time they entered the tabernacle courtyard.

We should always look to see if anything is missing from the story. As I went over this rebellion from the beginning, I noticed a few things missing. I don't know about you, but for me, one of the most difficult things to notice is what is *not* there.

Look to see if anything is missing from the story

Numbers 16 began by stating that Korah, 250 community leaders, and "Dathan and Abiram, sons of Eliab, and On son of Peleth" rebelled against Moses. So what happened to On? My hope was that On got it. That he recognized his error, brought his sin offering and went on to live a long life. The problem with my theory is that On is mentioned *nowhere* else in Scripture. That includes the census in Numbers 26.

"And the sons of Pallu: Eliab. The sons of Eliab: Nemuel, Dathan, and Abiram. These are the Dathan and Abiram, chosen from the congregation, who contended against Moses and Aaron in the company of Korah" (Numbers 26:8–9).

On is mentioned in a midrash. A midrash is like an ancient Jewish Bible commentary. This midrash says that On's wife got him drunk then sat outside of their tent with her hair hanging down. At that time, a woman was supposed to keep her hair covered. Having her hair uncovered meant she was rebelling against her husband. When Korah and his men came for On and saw his wife, they decided to stay out of the family dispute and forget about On. His wife's actions saved On, herself, and their children.[82] While this is a great story, there is no way of knowing if it is true.

The reality is far less interesting. Basically, On is the ancient equivalent of a typo. Instead of saying "Dathan and Abiram, sons of Eliab, and On son of Peleth," in Numbers 16:1, it should read "Dathan and Abiram, sons of Eliab, son of *Pallu*." That is the name given for Eliab's father in the census found in Numbers 26.

With this on my mind, God woke me around 3:00 a.m. It has become my custom to pray while waiting to fall back asleep. I was still at the top of my list, praying for my grandchildren, when God began to speak to me about Eleazar. He pointed out to me something very obvious; yet I almost missed it. This is another one of those things that is *not* there.

Since I have a hard time remembering things when I am awake, I felt the need to go to my computer before I forgot what God had to say. I pulled socks on my always freezing feet and turned on the space heater. Despite it being early May, West Michigan is looking at a high temperature of forty degrees for the day. I put my neck brace on, which corrects my posture and helps to keep headaches at bay. I fire up my computer. I listen, and I type. (God has called me to do many hard things in my life. At this point I do not consider getting up at 3:00 a.m. to be one of them.)

Eleazer had to do a hard thing. An extremely difficult thing.

And he did it.

Without complaining.

Or comparing.

God pointed out to me that *Eleazar was everything that Korah was not*. He did not complain about the job God called him to do. He did not ask why his brother Ithamar was not given this job. Or why Ithamar could not at least help him. Why is it we only seem to focus on the ones not doing their jobs?

> Contentment comes from knowing that God sees our obedience.

We might not always notice the obedient, but God does. Contentment comes from knowing God sees our obedience. God always rewards the obedient, perhaps in this lifetime, but definitely in the next. When this group finally reaches the Promised Land, Joshua and Caleb are not the only ones of their generation to enter. With them is Eleazar, the next high priest.

When the Israelites finally reached Moab, across the Jordan River from the city of Jericho, God commanded Moses and Eleazar to take a census. They recorded every man's age twenty and older who was able to fight in Israel's army. They began with the tribe of Reuben, but they did not get far before they reached Eliab, father to Nemuel, Dathan, and Abiram. Listing dead men in a census is weird. And if you recall, if it is weird, it is probably important.

The census then dedicates three verses to give a quick overview as to how Dathan and Abiram died. When you see anything other than names in a census, pay attention! We actually learn something about the rebellion that was not included in the account found in Numbers 16.

I will leave you with this: “The line of Korah, however, did not die out” (Numbers 26:11 NIV).

Digging Deeper

Read Numbers 11, paying attention to verses 1–3 and 34. What happens after these incidents that does not happen after Korah's rebellion?[83] Why do you think God treated this incident differently?

Self-Discovery

What does John 15:9–12 say is a benefit of our obedience to God?

According to 2 John 6, how do we show our love to God?

PART FIVE

The Results

(Numbers 16:41–17:13)

Chapter 21

The Next Day

While we have spent a considerable amount of time looking into the details of Korah's rebellion, it is important to remember that these events actually happened in quick succession. On the first day of the rebellion, Korah and his fellow rebels confronted Moses. God's judgment, which we just studied, took place on the second day. Today is the third day. A day to start anew!

The earth, which split open for the very first time, closed up again.
The ashes of the wannabe priests have been removed from the camp.
The sound of hammers rings out as the flattened censers are placed over the bronze altar.
The dust has settled, and God is giving Israel a fresh start:

But on the next day all the congregation of the people of Israel grumbled against Moses and against Aaron, saying, "You have killed the people of the LORD." And

> when the congregation had assembled against Moses and against Aaron, they turned toward the tent of meeting. And behold, the cloud covered it, and the glory of the LORD appeared. And Moses and Aaron came to the front of the tent of meeting, and the LORD spoke to Moses, saying, "Get away from the midst of this congregation, that I may consume them in a moment." And they fell on their faces. (Numbers 16:41–45)

The. Next. Day.

There is that word *but* again at the beginning of this passage, signaling a contrast. Here the contrast is between a fresh start and yet another rebellion. Number twelve, if you are counting.

What is wrong with these people? In Numbers 16:19, Korah gathered the entire congregation to rebel against Moses and Aaron. God showed grace in not killing each and every one of them! In His mercy, it was only those closely connected to the revolt who died. Remember, this happened just the previous day.

Though the instigators are dead, evidently the spirit of rebellion is still alive and well.

This time, though, it is the entire congregation rebelling, not just a few men. They are blaming Moses and Aaron for actions only God can perform. Can they possibly believe that Moses caused the land, which just happened to be beneath the tents of Dathan, Abiram, and Korah, to split apart and close back up again? Do they think it was Aaron who caused the 250 leaders to be reduced to ashes? They just do not get it. And did you catch how they referred to Korah and his fellow rebels? They called them the "people of the LORD!" (verse 41). This implies they agree with Korah's complaint and feel it was valid.[84]

On this day, God's presence appeared over the tent of meeting before Moses and Aaron even had time to turn around. They immediately came to its entrance and fell on their faces before God. Once again, they were pleading that God would spare His people. God spoke the exact same words He said in regard to Korah's rebellion. He warned Moses and Aaron to separate themselves from the crowd, so He could wipe out everyone else. Immediately!

I am amazed at Moses' and Aaron's dedication to this group of people—people who have caused them nothing but trouble. We see no hesitation as they rush to the tabernacle and prostrate themselves before God, praying the congregation would not be wiped out. Think of how difficult it is to keep forgiving the same action over and over again. It is only with God's help that they are able to do this.

In Korah's rebellion, Moses asked God if He was going to punish the whole group because of the sins of a few. But Moses cannot say that this time. Now it *is* the whole group rising up against God's chosen leaders.[85]

> And Moses said to Aaron, "Take your censer, and put fire on it from off the altar and lay incense on it and carry it quickly to the congregation and make atonement for them, for wrath has gone out from the LORD; the plague has begun." So Aaron took it as Moses said and ran into the midst of the assembly. And behold, the plague had already begun among the people. And he put on the incense and made atonement for the people. And he stood between the dead and the living, and the plague was stopped. (Numbers 16:46–48)

Aaron quickly offers God incense to make atonement for the people. "The English word 'atonement' comes from an Anglo-Saxon word, 'onement,' with the preposition 'at.' This literally means 'at-onement' or 'at unity.'"[86] Aaron offers incense on behalf of the people so that God will forgive their sins. In receiving the incense offering, God washes away the sin of the people and allows them to start over with a clean slate. Again. Here we find yet another example of God's grace.

In the Bible there is a connection between incense and prayer. The Psalmist says, "Let my prayer be counted as incense before you, and the lifting up of my hands as the evening sacrifice!" (Psalm 141:2). In the book of Revelation, the apostle John is given a vision of heaven. In it, he saw the twenty-four elders fall "down before the Lamb (that is, Jesus). Each one had a harp and they were holding golden bowls full of incense, which are the prayers of God's people" (Revelation 5:8 NIV). The smoke of the incense rising up from Aaron's censer acted as a prayer to stop God's punishment.[87]

When we see a man running in the Bible, we should always look to see **why** he is running.

Did you notice that Aaron did not walk, but ran to the group of rebels? At this time, in this culture, respectable men did not run. *Ever*. To do so, he would have had to gather up his tunic so he would not trip. This would cause his bare legs to show. "In that culture, it was humiliating and shameful for a man to show his bare legs."[88]

When we see a man running in the Bible, we should always look to see *why* he is running. Here, Aaron is running because this situation requires immediate action.[89] The longer it takes Aaron to burn the incense, the more people will die. Notice how Moses and Aaron are working together. God speaks only to Moses. Moses then passes the message on to Aaron. As high priest, Aaron is the only one who can offer incense to make atonement for the sins of the nation. Moses does not attempt to offer incense to God, and Aaron does not complain that all of God's words come to him through

Moses. We become content as we focus on the gifts and tasks God has given to us, rather than what He has given to others.

> We become content as we focus on the gifts and tasks God has given us.

But sin is not without penalty. After Aaron's offering, the plague stopped, but not before another 14,700 people died. As before, I do not think these are random deaths. I believe it was the people stirring up trouble who died. This grumbling was spreading through the community like wildfire. It became necessary to destroy the guilty so the nation could survive.[90]

Maybe now Moses and Aaron can lead the people in peace.

It is so easy to say, "I cannot believe these people still do not get it. Why in the world don't they change their behavior? By now they must know how severe the consequences will be." But behavior is a difficult thing to change. How often do we do the same thing, albeit on a smaller scale?

"I'm going to spend more time with God." But on the next day . . .

"I'm going to start eating healthier." But on the next day . . .

"I'm going to spend less time on technology." But on the next day . . .

Digging Deeper

Read the passages below. Who is running, and why?

Genesis 33:1–4

Luke 15:11–20

Do you think these two passages are connected? Why or why not?

Self-Discovery

Moses and Aaron do not take the actions of the Israelites personally. Instead, they ask God to forgive them. Have you ever asked God to forgive someone who hurt you?

How difficult is it for you to keep forgiving the same offense?

Have you asked for God's help?

List the gifts and the tasks God has given to you. How are you using those gifts?

How would you finish this sentence?

"I'm going to ______________________________." But on the next day . . .

Chapter 22

The Staff

Have you noticed the unhealthy pattern that has developed among the Israelites? First, Korah and his associates rebel against the leadership of Moses and Aaron. Then God brings judgment upon the rebels. Next, the entire community rebels against Moses and Aaron. Once again, God brings judgment. Now God is going to break this cycle by acting before the people have a chance to rebel again. He will announce His chosen spiritual leader to settle the matter once and for all.

> The LORD said to Moses, "Speak to the Israelites and get twelve staffs from them, one from the leader of each of their ancestral tribes. Write the name of each man on his staff. On the staff of Levi write Aaron's name, for there must be one staff for the head of each ancestral tribe. Place them in the tent of meeting in front of the ark of the covenant law, where I meet with you. The staff belonging to the man I choose will sprout, and I will rid myself of this constant grumbling against you by the Israelites." (Numbers 17:1–5 NIV)

Evidently, God has heard all the grumbling from these people that He cares to hear. Notice that last verse. God wants to rid Himself of the grumbling against Moses and Aaron. If God feels this way, imagine how His servants Moses and Aaron must have felt. Pushing a man to his limits is one thing. Pushing God to His limits is quite another!

Each tribal leader already had a staff, which represented his tribe and his authority in that tribe. While it could be used as a walking stick, it also comes in handy while herding sheep.[91] The staffs of Egyptian leaders were designed to represent themselves.[92] Since the Israelites recently left Egypt, it is possible that Israelite leaders followed Egypt's example and personalized their staffs too.

The word translated staff here is the Hebrew word *mattah*. A Bible dictionary can provide a greater understanding of the words of Scripture. Interestingly, while *mattah* means "rod" or "scepter," it can also be translated as "tribe."[93] This can literally mean "the 'descendants' or 'the tribe descended from a man' . . . When legs and feet are also mentioned, the staff between the legs also signifies . . . the male organ."[94] We see an example of this in Jacob's deathbed blessing of his son Judah: "The scepter shall not depart from Judah nor the ruler's staff from between his feet" (Genesis 49:10).

A Bible dictionary can provide a greater understanding of the words of Scripture.

Each tribal chief, including Aaron, handed Moses their staff. Moses then placed them before the Lord in front of the ark of the covenant, as God instructed. The ark is located in the Most Holy Place inside of the tent of meeting. This tent is also referred to as the tent of the testimony, or the tabernacle proper.[95] Only the high priest, Aaron at this point in time, is allowed to enter the Most Holy Place. And this is only allowed once a year, on the Day of Atonement.

However, Scripture tells us God met with Moses above the ark of the covenant. In fact, God gave Moses all the commands for the Israelites there. "When Moses entered the tent of meeting to speak with the LORD, he heard the voice speaking to him from between the two cherubim above the atonement cover on the ark of the covenant law" (Numbers 7:89 NIV). Some scholars say Moses must have been in the Holy Place, just outside of the Most Holy Place. But if God told Moses to put all of the leader's staffs in front of the ark, He could have allowed him to do just that, entering the Most Holy Place to do so.

To reach the Most Holy Place, Moses first entered the Holy Place. On his left is the golden lampstand. The Hebrew word for lampstand is *menorah.* Unlike the menorahs found in Jewish homes today, the menorah in the Holy Place was much larger. Although no one knows its size, according to Jewish tradition it is estimated to be about five feet tall.[96] It burned olive oil instead of candles and was made using seventy-five pounds of pure gold. The cups on the branches were "shaped like almond flowers with buds and blossoms" (Exodus 25:34 NIV).

> On the next day Moses went into the tent of the testimony, and behold, the staff of Aaron for the house of Levi had sprouted and put forth buds and produced blossoms, and it bore ripe almonds. Then Moses brought out all the staffs from before the LORD to all the people of Israel. And they looked, and each man took his staff. (Numbers 17:8–9)

The. Next. Day.

This next day was far different from the previous one. This time, there was no rebellion. God made it abundantly clear that Aaron was His chosen spiritual leader. In Numbers 17:5, God said the staff belonging to His chosen leader would sprout. But God did far more than that. Aaron's staff, a dead piece of wood, not only sprouted, but also had buds and flowers and ripe almonds!

The other staffs? Nothing.

Did you notice the resemblance between the branches of the *menorah* and Aaron's staff? In Israel, the almond tree signals that spring is near since it is one of the first trees to blossom. God chose to produce buds and flowers and almonds on Aaron's staff to emphasize that Aaron was his first choice for High Priest.[97]

The Hebrew word for almond comes from a root word that points to watchfulness, because of those early blossoms. "The almond blossoms on Aaron's staff imply that God was watching out against opposition toward the priest (Aaron) whom he had chosen."[98]

There is no denying that this is a work of God. Normally, a tree has buds. The buds open up into flowers. Then from the flowers come almonds. These normally appear one after the other, *never all at once.* And dead wood never does anything but deteriorate. By growing sprouts, buds, flowers, and almonds, it is as if God is saying, "I chose Aaron." "I choose Aaron!" "I WILL CHOOSE AARON!"

"And the LORD said to Moses, 'Put back the staff of Aaron before the testimony, to be kept as a sign for the rebels, that you may make an end of their grumblings against me, lest they die'" (Numbers 17:10).

In Exodus 16:33–34, God instructed Moses to have Aaron put manna in a jar and place it in the ark of the covenant. While giving the directions for building the ark, Exodus 25:16 records that the tablets listing the ten commandments were also to be placed there. Now they will be joined by Aaron's staff.

"The Israelites said to Moses, 'We will die! We are lost, we are all lost! Anyone who even comes near the tabernacle of the LORD will die. Are we all going to die?'" (Numbers 17:12–13 NIV).

Is your focus on God and the great things He has done?

Once again, we see the Israelites twisting facts, exaggerating, and going to extremes. At the beginning of Korah's rebellion, the rebels thought they all should be able to offer incense to God. That they were all holy. Now, they are doing just the opposite. They believe they are all going to die if they come anywhere near the tabernacle. "Their focus was still on themselves instead of on the Lord's gracious acts."[99]

Digging Deeper

Read Exodus 16:31–36. Why do you think God chose these items, plus Aaron's staff, to be kept?

Self-Discovery

When you *first* read Numbers 17:8, did it stand out to you that buds, blossoms, and fruit are never on a tree at the same time?

Can you think of something in your life that could have only come from God, but you didn't notice it at the time?

Describe where your focus is right now. Is it on God and all the great things He has done? Or is it on yourself and your weaknesses and limitations?

If your answer is the latter, what steps can you take to change your focus?

Chapter 23

The Line

I find it interesting that the book of Numbers alternates between events in the desert and sections of laws. The chapters following the miracle of Aaron's staff, Numbers 18 and 19, revert back to lessons about the law.[100] The Israelites' adventures in the desert continue in Numbers 20. The Israelites make it *one whole verse* before we hear about another rebellion.

"Now there was no water for the congregation. And they assembled themselves together against Moses and against Aaron. And the people quarreled with Moses and said, "Would that we had perished when our brothers perished before the Lord!" (Numbers 20:2–3).

Content people do not live in the past.

Here go the Israelites, flinging the back of their hands onto their foreheads again as they dramatically say, "If only we had died!" Content people do not say, "If only!" Content people do not live in the past.

If you think the phrase, "our brothers" is referring to Korah's rebellion, you would be correct. The Israelites are wishing they could have died with those men or in the plague. How is that for gratitude? Welcome to rebellion number thirteen.

But we are not going to focus on this or any other rebellions. (Yes, there are more.) Instead, we are going to pick up from where we left off in chapter 20 of *Enough*, where we were told, "the line of Korah, however, did not die out" (Numbers 26:11 NIV). Talk about a cliffhanger!

Here is another grace sighting. The families of Dathan and Abiram all died. While we are not told how many of Korah's sons survived, at least one of them did. And one is all it takes to continue the family line.

Sometimes studying the Bible can be like working a jigsaw puzzle. First, you need to find all the pieces. Then you can start sorting through them. An exhaustive Bible concordance can help us find many of the pieces to our puzzle concerning Korah's descendants.

An exhaustive Bible concordance can help us find many of the pieces to our puzzle.

Many study Bibles have a brief concordance in the back. While this can be helpful, it does not give us a complete listing. However, an exhaustive Bible concordance contains an alphabetical list of every single word in the Bible. And it turns out that Korah's name comes up quite a bit.

First Chronicles 6 has two genealogies that include Korah. One starts with his father Kohath (verse 1) and goes down through the generations. The other starts with "Heman the singer" (verse 33) and goes back in time to Kohath, son of Levi.

Following genealogies in the Bible can get complicated. While the two genealogies appear to have some differences, most of those differences can be explained. For instance, "son of" can literally refer to a son, but it can also mean a descendant. And there are times when multiple generations of people are skipped altogether.

In some instances, the names in the two lists do not appear to match. My husband is named Robert, but that is only used for official documents and by telemarketers. Almost everyone calls him Bob. Only his dad and his childhood Sunday school teacher called him Bobby. Some of the unmatching names in the censuses look like they may fall into this category.

Bob had a bit of a puzzle in his family tree. No one could figure out why his great-grandmother was called Carrie when she was given the good Dutch name Geertruida. I had an aunt with the same name, and she was called Gert. At least that made sense.

We finally found the answer in a letter written by Carrie's husband Nicholas. His request for military disability payments was denied because they thought he had two wives. In his response, Nick explained that he did not have two wives, but one wife with two names.

Nick went on to write that when Geertruida was young, her family, like many others, immigrated to Iowa. Her schoolteacher, unable (or unwilling) to pronounce the Dutch names, just gave the students new ones. "You will be Susan. You will be Joe. And you will be Carrie." And so, for the rest of her life, she was Carrie.

> These are the men whom David put in charge of the service of song in the house of the Lord after the ark rested there. They ministered with song before the tabernacle of the tent of meeting until Solomon built the house of the Lord in Jerusalem, and they performed

> their service according to their order. These are the men who served and their sons. Of the sons of the Kohathites: Heman the singer the son of Joel, son of Samuel, son of Elkanah, son of Jeroham. (1 Chronicles 6:31–34)

If you are familiar with the Bible, you may have recognized the name Samuel, son of Elkanah in the genealogy above. Let's read more about this family:

> There was a certain man of Ramathaim-zophim of the hill country of Ephraim whose name was Elkanah the son of Jeroham . . . He had two wives. The name of the one was Hannah, and the name of the other, Peninnah. And Peninnah had children, but Hannah had no children. (1 Samuel 1:1–2)

At first glance, it appears that Elkanah belongs to the tribe of Ephraim. That could imply that he was not a Levite. But if we continue reading 1 Chronicles 6, we learn this: "some of the clans of the sons of Kohath had cities of their territory out of the tribe of Ephraim" (1 Chronicles 6:66).

Like Reuben, brothers Simeon and Levi were also cursed by their father. These men were all sons of Jacob's unloved wife Leah. These brothers had a sister named Dinah. While the family was camped outside of town, the prince of that region, Shechem, forced himself on her. Shechem wanted to marry her, and the men of Shechem also wanted to intermarry with other women traveling with Jacob.

Dinah's brothers said they would allow this only if every man in the city was circumcised first. Shechem and his men agreed to this. But three days later, while they were still healing from the procedures, Simeon and Levi returned with weapons. They killed every man in the city while those men were unable to fight back. Then they took their sister Dinah and brought her back with them (see Genesis 34).

In Genesis 49:7, Jacob ended his curse on Simeon and Levi with these words: "Cursed be their anger, for it is fierce, and their wrath, for it is cruel! I will divide them in Jacob and *scatter them in Israel*" (emphasis added). It is because of this curse that the Levites were not given a territory of their own. Instead, they were given cities within the territories of the other tribes.

Elkanah is a descendent of Levi. Unlike Bob's great-grandpa Nick, Elkanah literally did have two wives. Every year, the family traveled to the tabernacle in Shiloh to celebrate feasts to the Lord. For many years, Hannah prayed for a child.

One year while in Shiloh, Hannah made a vow to God. She prayed, "O LORD of hosts, if you will indeed look on the affliction of your servant and remember me and not forget your servant, but will give to your servant a son, then I will give him to the LORD all the days of his life" (1 Samuel 1:11). Later, Hannah bore a son and named him Samuel, which means "name of God."[101]

Just as she promised, when Samuel was weaned, Hannah brought him to Eli, the priest at Shiloh. Samuel began hearing from God at an early age. "Samuel continued to grow both in stature and in favor with the LORD and also with man" (1 Samuel 2:26).

"Samuel grew, and the LORD was with him, and He fulfilled everything Samuel prophesied. All Israel from Dan to Beer-sheba knew that Samuel was a confirmed prophet of the LORD" (1 Samuel 3:19–20 HCSB).

As a prophet, Samuel relayed messages from God to the people. After Moses died in the desert, Joshua led the Israelites into the promised land. When Joshua died, God lead Israel through a series of judges. Samuel was the last judge in Israel before the people rejected God's leadership. They wanted a king like the neighboring nations.

I wonder if they began their request with the words, "If only . . . ?"

Digging Deeper

Compare the Levites actions in Genesis 34:1–29 with their actions in Exodus 32:25–29. How were their actions similar?

How are these two events different?

Self-Discovery

Is there something in your past that God wants you to let go of?

If so, what will be your first step?

Chapter 24

The Legacy

God is the King of Israel. He spoke to the nation through His prophets and ruled through His judges. Samuel was a prophet and Israel's last judge. Unfortunately, Samuel's sons were not leadership material. But that did not mean that God could not raise up someone else to serve as judge. However, the people did not want another judge. They wanted a king.

Like everyone else.

So all the elders of Israel gathered together and went to Samuel at Ramah. They said to him, "Look, you are old, and your sons do not follow your example. Therefore, appoint a king to judge us the same as all the other nations have."

When they said, "Give us a king to judge us," Samuel considered their demand sinful, so he prayed to the LORD. But the LORD told him, "Listen to the people and everything they say to you. They have not rejected you; they have rejected Me as their king." (1 Samuel 8:4–7 HCSB)

Look closely. According to Samuel, the people did not ask for a king. They demanded a king! With God as their leader, no other nation had an advantage over Israel. So why would the people of Israel want a king? Because everyone else had one.

Comparison is a contentment killer!

Comparison is a contentment killer! The Israelites were not focused on God and all He had done for them. They were looking around and longing for a ruler like the other nations had. They were not looking at Samuel's lifetime of faithful service to God. Instead, they were focused on the shortcomings of Samuel's sons. God points out that the people were not rejecting Samuel. They were rejecting God Himself!

God warns the people what will happen if they have an earthly king, but they ignore His advice. Have you ever heard the saying, "Be careful what you ask for, because you just might get it?" The Israelites will soon find out that having an earthly king is not all it is cracked up to be. God gives Israel an earthly king, not because it would be best for them, but because they insisted on it. Have you ever received something you insisted on, only to find out that was the wrong thing to ask for?

God instructs Samuel to anoint Saul as king over Israel. Saul's qualifications? He was tall, dark, and handsome (1 Samuel 9:2). Why follow the wisdom of God when there is someone good-looking to follow? As you might imagine, having Saul as king is a disaster. While Saul is still king, God instructs Samuel to anoint David, a young shepherd, as Saul's replacement. David did not become king immediately. It is estimated there were fifteen years between shepherd-boy David's anointing and the start of King David's reign.[103]

It is not unusual to have a length of time between God's calling and the fulfillment of that call. For instance, I first became aware of Korah's story from an issue of "Discipleship Journal" back in 2005.

There was a short, quarter-page article with an illustration of a lyre and a few Bible verses. As I dug into the Scriptures, I realized I would write this book. But there were eighteen years between when I was called to write this book and when I was qualified to write this book.

Shortly after David's anointing, he fought and killed the giant Goliath. Saul became jealous of David and tried to kill him on multiple occasions, so David went on the run. All of the years spent guiding sheep in the desert equipped David to evade Saul and his murderous army.

In the years between David's anointing and becoming king, men gathered around him and formed an army. They came to be known as David's mighty men. "They were bowmen and could shoot arrows and sling stones with either the right or the left hand . . . Elkanah, Isshiah, Azarel, Joezer, and Jashobeam, the Korahites" (1 Chronicles 12:2, 6) were among David's mighty men. So, in addition to Samuel, some of the brave men who fought alongside David were also descendants of Korah.

1426 BC	1100 BC	1010 BC	1000 BC[104]
Korah's Rebellion	Samuel born	Korahites David's Mighty Men	Musicians in Jerusalem

While Saul ruled Israel, the tabernacle stayed in the city of Shiloh, which is located in the territory of Ephraim. After David became king, the tabernacle was moved to Jerusalem. Because the tabernacle was now stationary, the job description of the descendants of Korah evolved. They kept their job as guards, but instead of being moving men, they became musicians.

There was a great celebration when the ark of the covenant came to Jerusalem!

> David also commanded the chiefs of the Levites to appoint their brothers as the singers who should play loudly on musical instruments, on harps and lyres and cymbals, to raise sounds also of joy. So the Levites appointed Heman the son of Joel (son of Samuel); and of his brothers Asaph the son of Berechiah . . . The singers, Heman, Asaph, and Ethan, were to sound bronze cymbals. (1 Chronicles 15:16–17, 19)

David wanted to build a permanent dwelling place for God. He even drew up the plan for a temple according to God's instructions. But God did not want David to build the temple. David was a warrior and as such, had blood on his hands. Instead, the honor of building God's temple in Jerusalem fell to David's son Solomon:

> As for the divisions of the gatekeepers: of the Korahites, Meshelemiah the son of Kore . . . These divisions of the gatekeepers, corresponding to their chief men, had duties, just as their brothers did, ministering in the house of the Lord. And they cast lots by fathers' houses, small and great alike, for their gates. The lot for the east fell to Shelemiah. (1 Chronicles 26:1, 12–14)

Casting lots was a way of determining what God wanted. Proverbs 16:33 says, "The lot is cast into the lap, but its every decision is from the Lord." If we look at the diagram of the tabernacle[105] (which also applies to the temple) we see Shelemiah and his family were assigned to guard the side of the temple with the gate. God assigned the descendants of Korah the most respected position. Rather than being known as rebels like their ancestor Korah, the family now has a respectable reputation.

1426 BC	1100 BC	1010 BC	1000 BC	979 BC[106]
Korah's Rebellion	Samuel born	Korahites David's Mighty Men	Musicians in Jerusalem	Shelemiah Gatekeeper

After the reign of King Solomon, the nation of Israel split in two—Israel to the north, and Judah (and the temple) to the south. Unfortunately, *every* king of Israel was wicked. After 200 years, God sent judgment on them. They were conquered and taken captive by the nation of Assyria. The nation of Judah had some good kings mixed in with the bad. One of the good kings was Hezekiah. He began his reign in Judah just after Israel was taken captive.

A Bible timeline helps to put events in chronological order.

Did you know that the Bible is not all in chronological order? The Bible is arranged the way it is for a reason, but sometimes, such as when tracing a family line, it is helpful to know the order in which events occurred. A Bible timeline helps to put events in chronological order.

When Hezekiah became king, about 275 years after David,[107] the temple was in a sorry state of neglect. King Hezekiah called in Levites to restore and consecrate the temple. "Then the Levites arose, Mahath the son of Amasai, and Joel the son of Azariah, of the sons of the Kohathites" (2 Chronicles 29:12). They worked with Levites descended from Merari and Gershon. "They gathered their brothers and consecrated themselves and went in as the king had commanded, by the words of the LORD, to cleanse the house of the LORD" (2 Chronicles 29:15).

Judah existed over 100 years before they, too, were judged by God. They were defeated and taken captive by the Babylonians. Then, after seventy years of exile in Babylon, something miraculous happened. The captives from Judah were allowed to return to Jerusalem!

"Thus says Cyrus king of Persia: The Lord, the God of heaven, has given me all the kingdoms of the earth, and he has charged me to build him a house at Jerusalem . . . Whoever is among you of all his people, may his God be with him, and let him go up to Jerusalem . . . and rebuild the house of the Lord, the God of Israel." (Ezra 1:2–3)

King Cyrus not only allowed the captives to return to Jerusalem; he told them to rebuild the temple. He even returned all the items that King Nebuchadnezzar had taken from the temple years earlier.

1426 BC . . .	1010 BC	1000 BC	979 BC	716 BC	457 BC[108]
Korah's Rebellion	Korahites David's Mighty Men	Musicians in Jerusalem	Shelemiah Gatekeeper	Mahath & Joel Cleanse Temple	Shallum Gatekeeper

> Now the first to resettle on their own property in their own towns were some Israelites, priests, Levites and temple servants . . . Shallum son of Kore, the son of Ebiasaph, the son of Korah, and his fellow gatekeepers from his family (the Korahites) were responsible for guarding the thresholds of the tent just as their ancestors had been responsible for guarding the entrance to the dwelling of the Lord. (1 Chronicles 9:2, 19 NIV)

Almost 1,000 years after the rebellion, Korah's descendants are still serving God at the temple! "Mattithiah, one of the Levites, the firstborn of Shallum the Korahite, was entrusted with making the flat cakes. Also some of their kinsmen of the Kohathites had charge of the showbread, to prepare it every Sabbath" (1 Chronicles 9:31–32).

Digging Deeper

Who is the oldest ancestor that you know of? What do you know about their faith?

Self-Discovery

Have you ever received something you insisted on, only to find out that was the wrong thing to ask for? What did you ask for, and why was it the wrong thing?

In hindsight, what do you wish you had asked for?

Is there something you thought you would get instantly, but you had to wait a long time for? What did you do during your time of waiting?

Are you in a season of waiting right now? How can you be preparing for what is to come?

Chapter 25

The Psalms

As musicians, the descendants of Korah did not merely play instruments and sing songs. They also wrote songs, which we now call psalms. The book of Psalms was compiled sometime after Judah's exile in Babylon. But many of the psalms themselves were written earlier, during the reign of King David.

The book of Psalms is divided into five sections; each section is also called a book. Each book in the Psalms connects with the corresponding book in the Torah (the Hebrew name for the first five books of the Bible). Book One of the Psalms connects with the themes of Genesis, Book Two with Exodus, and so on.[109]

Book Two (Psalms 42–72) begins with psalms written by the "Sons of Korah," which refers to the descendants of the rebel Korah. Those psalms are followed by one written by Asaph. The remainder of the psalms in Book Two are written either by David or an unknown author.

Book Three of the Psalms parallels the book of Leviticus, which contains laws given by God to teach us how to be holy. This third book (Psalms 73–89) contains "expressions of worship . . . focused on God's instruction in holiness."[110] Interestingly, every psalm in Book Three is written by Levites with one exception: Psalm 86 is written by David.

I love order, and I believe that comes from my Heavenly Father. The first thing we see God doing in the Bible is bringing order out of chaos. We also get a glimpse of this order in the Psalms. Not only because of the connection between the Torah and the books of psalms, but also because of the order found in Book Three.

First Chronicles 6:31–47 says that after the ark came to Jerusalem, King David put three Levites in charge of worship music. Heman, son of Joel, represented the Kohathites. Asaph, descendant of Gershon, stood to Heman's right. Ethan, descendant of Merari, stood to Heman's left. So each of the three Levite clans was represented. The diagram below shows how the Levites stood as they led worship.

Asaph	Heman	Ethan
	. . . son of Korah,	
(Clan of Gershon)	(Clan of Kohath)	(Clan of Merari)
Book 2: Psalm 50	Book 2: Psalms 42–49	
Book 3: Psalms 73–83	Book 3: Psalms 84, 85, 87, 88	Book 3: Psalm 89

Now look at the order of the psalms they wrote in Book Three. We see them arranged in the Bible just like the worshippers saw the musicians standing in the tabernacle. Which is just one of the many reasons why I believe the Bible is the coolest book ever!

Did you know that the Bible was not divided into chapters and verses when it was first written? They were added much later, so that its parts could be referenced more easily. The headings we see in many Bibles are not part of Scripture either. However, the titles of the Psalms *are* considered to be a part of Scripture. In fact, in Hebrew Bibles the titles of the Psalms are labeled as verse one.[111]

The titles of the psalms composed by Asaph and Ethan do not mention their Levite ancestor. In contrast, the remaining Levite psalms do not mention the name of any individual. Instead, they refer to themselves as "the Sons of Korah." Given what we know about Korah, why would these psalmists want to be known as his descendants? They could have just signed their first name like the other psalmists. Or they could call themselves descendants of any ancestor from the previous 400 years.

Psalm 42 is the first psalm we find written by Korah's descendants. It begins like this: "To the Choirmaster. A maskil of the Sons of Korah." *Maskil* means "to have insight" or "to be skillful."[112] This psalm is a lament, which means "to express sorrow, mourning, or regret for, often demonstratively."[113]

As a deer pants for flowing streams,
so pants my soul for you, O God.
My soul thirsts for God, for the living God.
When shall I come and appear before God?
(Psalm 42:1–2)

The Sons of Korah were writing about their desire to serve in God's temple. There were very few Levites who served there full-time. Most Levites lived in cities scattered around Israel. In 1 Chronicles 25 the Levites are divided into twenty-four groups. Each group would travel to Jerusalem twice a year to serve in the temple for one week. In addition, all Levites came to Jerusalem to serve at Passover (Unleavened Bread), Pentecost (Weeks) and the Feast of Tabernacles (Booths). All Jews worldwide were encouraged to travel to Jerusalem to celebrate these three festivals. Extra Levites were needed to accommodate the crowds and their sacrifices. The authors of Psalm 42 look back on these festivals with fondness:

These things I remember, as I pour out my soul:
how I would go with the throng and lead them
in procession to the house of God
with glad shouts and songs of praise,
a multitude keeping festival. (Psalm 42:4)

We also find a contrast between the psalmist, who remembers God, and God, whom he thinks has forgotten him:

My soul is cast down within me; therefore *I remember you*
from the land of Jordan and of Hermon,
from Mount Mizar. (Psalm 42:6)

I say to God, my rock: "Why have *you forgotten me?*
Why do I go mourning because of the oppression of
the enemy?" (Psalm 42:9)

Psalm 43 is believed to be a continuation of Psalm 42. Psalm 43 does not have a title, and it repeats a verse found twice in Psalm 42:

Why are you cast down, O my soul,
and why are you in turmoil within me?
Hope in God; for I shall again praise him,
my salvation and my God. (Psalm 43:5)

You may not have heard of Korah before you picked up this book. Or you may have only known his name because you saw it in the Psalms. I think that is the way the descendants of Korah would have wanted it. Rather than be ashamed of the name of their rebellious ancestor, through their faithful service and the writing of psalms, the name has been redeemed. The name of Korah is no longer associated with rebels, but with worshippers. Calling themselves the "Sons of Korah" is a reminder of the transforming power of God's grace.

Like Psalm 42, Psalm 84 also begins with a desire to serve God at the temple. But this psalm is not a lament. It is a psalm of praise!

How lovely is your dwelling place, O Lord of hosts!
My soul longs, yes, faints for the courts of the Lord;
my heart and flesh sing for joy to the living God.
(Psalm 84:1–2)

The Sons of Korah realize that they only exist by the grace of God. They remember what took place in the desert so many years ago and how far their family has come. They now rejoice in the very tasks their ancestor rebelled against:

For a day in your courts is better
than a thousand elsewhere.
I would rather be a doorkeeper
in the house of my God
than dwell in the tents of wickedness. (Psalm 84:10)

Like the apostle Paul, the Sons of Korah have learned to be content, regardless of the circumstances (Philippians 4:12 NIV).

Digging Deeper

Read the following passages and record what they have to say about God's relationship with us:

Deuteronomy 31:6–8

Joshua 1:5–9

Psalm 139

Self-Discovery

Based on the words of Psalm 84, list any similarities or differences you find between Korah and his descendants.

Which words are true of you?

Which words would you like to ask God to make true for you?

Return to the questions asked at the end of the first chapter of this book. Were all your questions answered?

What can you add to what you know about the Israelites?

The Best News Ever!

The television series "Monk" follows the exploits of detective Adrian Monk. He was a police officer whose wife, Trudy, was killed by a car bomb. Monk believed that he, specifically his occupation, was somehow responsible for her death. He developed severe OCD and, unable to function, lost his job. Yet he was so skilled as a detective, he was called to work as a consultant for the police department. He had the ability to solve the cases no one else could. Except for one. He could not solve the case of his wife's murder.

In a flashback scene, we learn that Trudy left a gift for Monk and placed it under their Christmas tree just before she was killed. Year after year, Monk could not bring himself to open it. Unknown to Monk, that was a tragic mistake. You see, Trudy, a journalist, feared that the person she was investigating might be trying to kill her. So she recorded herself, explaining the story she was working on, who was involved, and what she suspected. She then gift-wrapped the recording and wrote Adrian's name on the tag. But because Monk did not open it, he lived for many years searching for answers that were in his grasp all along.

Many of us do the same thing. We may have heard about Jesus, but we don't know Him.

Jesus is God's gift to humanity. He is the Son of God, born to a young virgin named Mary over 2,000 years ago. He lived a life without sin. (He didn't do anything God said not to do). Not one lie, no jealousy, always doing the right thing. He lived exactly the way God wants all of us to live, something no mere human is able to do.

Although he was completely innocent, Jesus was insulted, beaten, and crucified—a horrific, painful death. Being God's son, He had the power to stop it at any time, but He did not. Jesus *allowed* Himself to be crucified and killed because He loves us—each and every one of us. On the third day, He rose from the dead, something only God can do!

God knows there is no way that anyone can be good enough to get into heaven. That is why Jesus took our place and received the punishment for our sin (offering us salvation). But this is not just about avoiding the eternal torment of hell and getting into heaven. It is also about starting a new life and having a relationship with God right now! This is a gift. The greatest gift we could ever be given, and it is offered to EVERYONE.

Monk's life was changed when he finally accepted Trudy's gift by opening it. Our lives will be changed when we accept the gift of salvation that comes through Jesus. It is yours for the asking. If you would like to spend eternity with God in heaven, and begin a new life now, pray (talk) to Him like the example below:

> God, please forgive me for all the wrong things I have done. (List the things you can remember. This is called confession). I believe Jesus is Your Son. I believe He is fully God and fully human. I believe He lived a perfect life. I believe He suffered, He died, and He was buried. I

> believe He rose from the dead, conquering death. Thank You for choosing me to be your child. Thank You for paying the penalty for my sin so I can spend eternity in heaven with You. Please help me to love You and Your Word and become more and more like Jesus. I pray this in Jesus' name, Amen.

If you prayed this prayer, welcome to the family of God! Write down this date and go and tell someone your good news! I was not planning to include this message in this book, so God placed this here for you, my friend! I would love to hear from you as well. You can find me online at LisaLewisKoster.com or on Facebook at LisaLewisKosterSpeaks.

For Continuing Study

Throughout this book I have been introducing tools that help us better understand the Bible. Now it is your turn to put them to use! If you are not sure where to start, I suggest studying the Psalms written by the Sons of Korah—Psalms 42–49, 84, 85, 87 and 88.

I like to mark things I find as I go, without marking up my Bible. I copy the Scripture passages onto my computer (you can find Bibles in various translations online), double space it and print it off. But recently I've discovered Scripture journals. There are sets containing the entire Bible, but you can also purchase just one book.

The "Illuminated Scripture Journal" by Crossway has a volume just for the Psalms. The text for each Psalm is printed and double-spaced on the left-hand page, while the page on the right is blank so you can write notes.

I find it easiest to start by looking for words that are repeated. I like to mark them with different shapes and colors. An internet search of "Inductive Bible study symbols" will give you some suggestions on how to mark different words, or you can make your own system.

Work through each Psalm using the tools introduced throughout the book. (Not every tool will apply). Then zoom out and look for repeated words, phrases, or themes among these Psalms. Finally, ask yourself, "What does this mean to me?" or "What is God asking me to do based on what I have read?"

May God give you an ever-increasing hunger for His Word!

Blessings,

Lisa

Tips for Small Group Leaders

First, thank you for leading a small group. If this is your first time leading, you can do this! Step one is always prayer (see Introduction). Invite God to lead you as you lead the group and pray for the members of your group.

This book was designed to work well as a six-week Bible study. Use your first meeting for introductions and an overview of the study. If you need some ideas for your first meeting, search the internet for "ice breakers." You may want to use a timer if you have a large group so everyone has an opportunity to share.

For an overview at your first meeting, I recommend reading Numbers 16:1–35 aloud. Reading in smaller sections works best (verses 1–3, 4–7, 8–11, 12–15, 16–19, 20–24, 25–27, 28–30 and 31–35). Rather than reading it all yourself, you may want to ask for volunteers. If you go around the group taking turns reading, give members a safe way to opt out. I like to say, "If anyone forgot their glasses or something, just nudge the person next to you, and they can pick up the reading." After each section ask, "What stands out to you?" or "What are your thoughts about this passage?"

Lay down some ground rules. Some of the questions in the study are personal. Group members should share only their own experiences and not mention anyone else by name. Stress that everything shared in the group is confidential and any comments should be respectful. Instruct each member to work through the first section (five chapters) of the book. Then, at your next meeting, discuss those chapters.

Be prepared. I suggest working at least a week ahead of the group. That way you're able to give specific instructions on what the group is about to study next. Plus, that gives you a built-in safety net. If something comes up unexpectedly, you'll still be prepared for the next lesson.

The Bible contains some very unfamiliar names. Listen to an audio Bible (found online) to hear the pronunciation. If all else fails, just say the name with confidence. The Old Testament is written in Hebrew, so it's doubtful we're pronouncing names correctly anyway.

Don't be afraid of silence. It seems longer than it really is. Give people time to wrestle with God if He's calling them to speak. Before you move on, rephrase the question and give it just a bit more time.

Be willing to jump in and redirect if someone is talking too long or going off-track. Look for an opening, then ask if anyone else has any thoughts on that topic or move on to the next question.

If you don't know the answer to a question, be honest. Open it up to the group and see if anyone else has an answer. If they don't, ask everyone in the group (including yourself) to look for the answer and start with that at your next meeting.

Don't worry about making mistakes. We all make them at some point. I once said "satan" when I should have said "God." That's got to be right up there on the list of errors! After I misspoke, the room went silent. I said, "Well that came out wrong," corrected myself, and moved on. In those moments, I tell myself, "In the scheme of all eternity, how important is my feeling stupid for ten minutes?"

If you're able, play the praise song "Better Is One Day" at your first and last meetings. The song's message becomes clearer after you have completed the last chapter in this book.

Finally, remember, God has this! He is far greater than all of our shortcomings.

Acknowledgments

So many people played a part in making this book a reality. Here are just a few who helped me on the journey that culminated in this book:

Kevin Harney, my first pastor and the first person to show me what to look for in the Bible. Thanks for pointing me to Jesus.

Nancy Bretschneider, thank you for your patience, understanding and guidance with this brand-new Christian. You helped me navigate following God and living abundantly despite chronic pain.

Cindy Bultema, thank you for bringing me into your fold and teaching me that we are all on the same team.

Kathy Bruins, thanks for making me a part of CSI and giving me the blessing of teaching at The Well conference each year. Thank you for seeing value in what God has called me to do.

Thank you to my Word Weavers group. You are worth the drive. Everything I write is so much better because of you!

Mary Cook, thank you for all your questions and for listening to my latest Bible discoveries.

Molly Dollahan-Gortsema, thanks for being a beta reader and sharing your insights despite your busy schedule. Shalom, shalom!

Tim Wilson, thank you for your encouragement, your valuable feedback, and for teaching me something new about the Bible almost every Sunday.

Lori Gesink and Kaylyn VanHarn, thanks for being guinea pigs, working through the study with me and giving your helpful feedback.

Cassie Peereboom and Ryan Nousen, thank you for all of your support. I love you to pieces and am so incredibly proud of you both!

Bob Koster, my husband of many years and my biggest cheerleader. You make my life, and me, so much better. I can't imagine where I'd be without you. Thanks!

Most of all, praise be to God who gave me what I could never earn. Thank you for calling me Yours and giving me a hunger and love for Your Word.

Notes

1. Bill T. Arnold and Bryan E. Beyer, "Failure in the Desert," in *Encountering the Old Testament, A Christian Survey,* ed. Walter A. Elwell and Eugene H. Merrill (Grand Rapids, MI: Baker Book House, 1999), 134.
2. Howard G. Hendricks and William D. Hendricks, *Living by the Book: The Art and Science of Reading the Bible* (Chicago: Moody Publishers, 1991), 33.
3. God changed Abram's name to Abraham in Genesis 17:5.
4. And people say the Bible is boring! You can read Joseph's story in Genesis 37–50.
5. -ite, Merriam-Webster Dictionary, https://www.merriam-webster.com/dictionary/-ite.
6. Robert L. Thomas, *New American Standard Hebrew-Aramaic and Greek Dictionaries: Updated Edition* (Anaheim: Foundation Publications, Inc., 1998).
7. J. D. Barry et al., *Faithlife Study Bible* (Bellingham, WA: Lexham Press, 2012, 2016), Numbers 1:46.
8. Barker and Kohlenberger, *The Expositor's Bible Commentary, Abridged Edition, Old Testament* (Grand Rapids, MI: Zondervan Academic, 2004), 173.
9. Benjamin Elisha Sawe, "The Largest Stadiums in the United States," WorldAtlas, January 19, 2020, https://www.worldatlas.com/articles/

which-are-the-largest-stadiums-in-the-united-states.html.

10. Thomas, *New American Standard Hebrew-Aramaic and Greek Dictionaries: Updated Edition*.
11. Pastor Tim Wilson, South Harbor Church, Byron Center, MI.
12. You will find some of these reporter's questions in italics in the previous chapters.
13. In addition to the Law, the Talmud includes something similar to what we call a commentary.
14. Timothy R. Ashley, *The Book of Numbers* (Grand Rapids, MI: William B. Eerdman's Publishing Company, 1993) 260–261.
15. Hendricks, *Living by the Book*, 91.
16. "Shampoo Commercial," posted by ConnectedtheBook, November 5, 2009, https://www.youtube.com/watch?v=brC_jK6stBs.
17. John D. Barry et al., *Faithlife Study Bible*, Exodus 19:6.
18. In study Bibles, a cross-reference is a tiny little letter above the words of Scripture, which we tend to ignore. In Numbers 16:3, "For aall in the congregation are holy," you will see a small "a" before the word "all." When you see this in a Bible, that letter will correspond with a reference to a book, chapter, and verse elsewhere within the Bible. In this case, that verse is found in Exodus 19:5–6. (Cross-references can vary between different Bible translations.)
19. See "The Best News Ever!" near the end of this book.
20. Barry, J. D., et al, *Faithlife Study Bible*, Numbers 16:4.
21. Ashley, "The Time Word Mahar as a Key to Transitional Development," in *The Book of Numbers*, 308.
22. Ashley, *The Book of Numbers*, 305.
23. Joy Gage, *Lord, Can We Talk This Over?* (Chicago, IL: Moody Bible Institute, 1980), 56.
24. Richard S. Hess, *Israelite Religions* (Grand Rapids, MI: Baker Academic, 2007), 156.
25. Pastor Tim Wilson, South Harbor Church.
26. Ray VanderLaan, "The Road to the Cross" lecture, Providence Christian Reformed Church, Grand Rapids, MI, March 24, 2017.
27. VanderLaan, "The Road to the Cross."
28. See *Enough* chapter 5.
29. Pastor Tim Wilson, South Harbor Church.

30. "Tabernacle," in *Holman Christian Standard Bible*, HCSB Bullet Notes (Nashville, TN: Holman Bible Publishers, 2010), 2236.
31. "There is some evidence for the use of 'Gad' as an epithet meaning '(god of) good fortune' for various gods and goddesses in Syria and Palestine. 'Dan' with the meaning 'ruler, judge,' may have been the title of a Canaanite deity. 'Asher' may be a masculine counterpart of Asherah. 'Zebulun' recalls the name 'Baal-zebul.' All this remains mere speculation, but in any case, the process of assimilation and integration began very early, before the Palestinian Israelites became acquainted with Yahwism." Georg Fohrer, History of Israelite Religion (Nashville, New York: Abingdon Press, 1972), 39–41, 64–65.
32. Ray VanderLaan, lecture at Baker Book House, September 29, 2006.
33. Ray VanderLaan, "The Desert: How Big is your God?" lecture at Friendship Christian Reformed Church, Byron Center, MI, July 31, 2003.
34. Hendricks, *Living by the Book*, 152–155.
35. Brad Adgate, "Agencies Agree; 2021 Was A Record Year For Ad Spending, With More Growth Expected In 2022," Forbes, December 8, 2021, https://www.forbes.com/sites/bradadgate/2021/12/08/agencies-agree-2021-was-a-record-year-for-ad-spending-with-more-growth-expected-in-2022/?sh=3bc2422b7bc6.
36. "Grumble," Dictionary.com, accessed August 1, 2023, https://www.dictionary.com/browse/grumble.
37. "Murmur," Dictionary.com, accessed August 1, 2023, https://www.dictionary.com/browse/murmur.
38. "Complain," Dictionary.com, accessed August 1, 2023, https://www.dictionary.com/browse/grumble.
39. Farlex, "Kvetching," The Free Dictionary, accessed August 1, 2023, https://www.thefreedictionary.com/kvetching.
40. Ray VanderLaan, interview by author, Providence Christian Reformed Church, Grand Rapids, MI, March 25, 2017.
41. Bob Mumford, "Agape Road: Journey to Intimacy with the Father," Lifechangers, 2002, VHS.
42. Such as in Exodus 20:4-5; 34:6–7.
43. See Leviticus 20:11.

44. Ashley, *The Book of Numbers*, 310.
45. Ashley, *The Book of Numbers*, 310.
46. Chad Brand et al., eds., "Gers hom," *Holman Illustrated Bible Dictionary* (Nashville, TN: Holman Bible Publishers, 2003), 640.
47. Ashley, *The Book of Numbers*, 311.
48. "MacLaren's Expositions, Judges, Strength Profaned and Lost," Bible Hub, https://biblehub.com/commentaries/judges/16-21.htm.
49. Baruch A. Levine, *The Anchor Bible: Numbers 1–20*, (New York: Doubleday, 1993), 414.
50. John Peter Lange et al., *A Commentary on the Holy Scriptures: Numbers* (Bellingham, WA: Logos Bible Software, 2008), 89.
51. Levine, The Anchor Bible, 414.
52. George Bush, *Notes Critical and Practical on the Book of Numbers.* (London: Forgotten Books, 2018), 236–237.
53. Chapter 10 lists the definitions of these words.
54. Roy Gane, "The Korah Rebellion," in *The NIV Application Commentary, Leviticus, Numbers* (Grand Rapids, MI: Zondervan, 2004) 635.
55. Levine, *The Anchor Bible*: Numbers 1–20, 414.
56. Barry et al., *Faithlife Study Bible*, Leviticus 10:1.
57. Ron Graham, "Nadab and Abihu—What Did They Do Wrong?" Simply Bible, https://www.simplybible.com/f077-warns-Nadab-and-abihu.htm.
58. "Pulpit Commentary," Bible Hub, https://biblehub.com/commentaries/pulpit/numbers/16.htm.
59. "Jamieson-Fausset-Brown Bible Commentary," Bible Hub, https://biblehub.com/commentaries/jfb/numbers/16.htm.
60. *Amplified Bible, Classic Edition* (Grand Rapids, MI: Zondervan Publishing House and the Lockman Foundation, 1987), Hebrews 13:5.
61. Tabernacle Graphic: John D. Hannah, "Exodus," in *The Bible Knowledge Commentary: An Exposition of the Scriptures*, ed. J. F. Walvoord and R. B. Zuck, vol. 1 (Wheaton, IL: Victor Books, 1985), 146.
62. "Egyptian God," Egyptian History, January 21, 2021, https://egyptian-history.com/blogs/egyptian-gods/egyptian-gods.
63. Tim Wilson, South Harbor Church.
64. Hannah, "Exodus," 102–103.

65. Robert L. Thomas, *New American Standard Hebrew-Aramaic and Greek Dictionaries: Updated Edition* (Anaheim: Foundation Publications, Inc., 1998).
66. Lois Tverberg, Walking in the Dust of Rabbi Jesus (Grand Rapids, MI: Zondervan, 2012), 211.
67. James F. Coakley, "Numbers," in *The Moody Bible Commentary*, ed. by Michael Rydelnik and Michael VanLaningham (Chicago: Moody Publishers, 2014), 238.
68. Matt Woodley. *The Gospel of Matthew: God with Us* (Downers Grove, IL: IVP Books, 2011), 198.
69. Thomas, *NAS Dictionaries*.
70. Schoolhouse Rock, "Conjunction Junction," https://genius.com/Schoolhouse-rock-conjunction-junction-lyrics.
71. Gane, *Korah Rebellion*, 635.
72. Walter Riggins, *Numbers: Daily Study Bible* (Philadelphia: The Westminster Press, 1983), 134–135.
73. Gordon Wenham, *Numbers: An Introduction and Commentary* (Downers Grove, IL: Inter-Varsity Press, 1981), 137–138.
74. Source unknown.
75. W. H. Bellinger, Jr., Leviticus and Numbers (*New International Biblical Commentary. Old Testament Series, 3*) (Peabody, MA: Hendrickson Publishers, 2001), 241.
76. Katherarine Doob Sakenfeld, *Journeying with God: A Commentary on the Book of Numbers* (International Theological Commentary), (Grand Rapids, MI: William B. Eerdman's Publishing Company, 1995), 101.
77. Ashley, *The Book of Numbers*, 318.
78. Illustration courtesy of Tim Wilson, South Harbor Church, 2023.
79. Gane, *Korah Rebellion*, 636.
80. Ibid.
81. Anastasia Boniface-Malle, "Numbers," in *Africa Bible Commentary*, ed. Tokunboh Adeyemo (Grand Rapids, MI: Zondervan, 2006), 189.
82. Chaim Bentorah, "Hebrew Word Study—On Son of Peleth," Chaim Bentorah Biblical Hebrew Studies, May 26, 2018, https://www.chaimbentorah.com/2018/05/hebrew-word-study-on-son-of-peleth/.

83. Answer: The site of Korah's rebellion is not given a name.
84. Dr. Alan Kurschner, "The Significance of the Golden Censer within the Prewrath Framework," Eschatos Ministries, December 16, 2020, https://www.alankurschner.com/2020/12/16/the-significance-of-the-golden-censer-within-the-prewrath-framework/.
85. Dennis T. Olson, Numbers, *Interpretation, A Bible Commentary for Teaching and Preaching* (Louisville: John Knox Press, 1996), 107.
86. "Atonement," in *The Baker Illustrated Bible Dictionary*, ed. Tremper Longman III (Grand Rapids, MI: Baker Books, 2013), 142-143.
87. Coakley, "Numbers," 239.
88. Matthew Williams, "The Prodigal Son's Father Shouldn't have Run," Biola Magazine, May 31, 2010, https://www.biola.edu/blogs/biola-magazine/2010/the-prodigal-sons-father-shouldnt-have-run.
89. John A Beck, "Run" in *The Baker Illustrated Guide to Everyday Life in Bible Times* (Grand Rapids, MI: Baker Publishing Group), 214.
90. Gage. Lord, Can We Talk This Over?, 82.
91. Coakley, "Numbers," 239.
92. *HCSB Study Bible: Holman Christian Standard Bible* (Nashville, TN: Holman Bible Publishers, 2010), 250.
93. Thomas, *NAS Dictionaries*, "staff."
94. Mary Douglas, *In the Wilderness, The Doctrine of Defilement in the Book of Numbers* (Sheffield: JSOT Press, 1993), 132-133.
95. See diagram of the tabernacle in Chapter 16: The Congregation.
96. *Rose Guide to the Tabernacle* (Peabody, Massachusetts: Rose Publishing LLC, 2008), 56.
97. Morris A. Inch, *Two Mosaic Motifs, Freedom Trek & Gentiles Are Us* (Lanham—New York—Oxford: University Press of America, Inc., 2003), 55.
98. Roy E. Gane, "Rebellion of Korah and Aftermath" in *The Baker Illustrated Bible Background Commentary*, ed. J. Scott Duvall and J. Daniel Hays (Grand Rapids, MI: Baker Publishing Group, 2020), 178.
99. Coakley, "Numbers," 239–240.
100. Douglas, *In the Wilderness*, 103.
101. Thomas, "Samuel," *NAS Dictionaries*.
102. "Bible Timeline," Bible Hub, https://biblehub.com/timeline/#ot.

103. "Introduction to 1 Samuel," in *Archeological Study Bible* (Grand Rapids, MI: Zondervan, 2005), 395.
104. "Bible Timeline," Bible Hub.
105. *Enough* chapter 16.
106. "Bible Timeline," Bible Hub.
107. "Chronology of Kings, Prophets, and Nations in the Old Testament," Biblical History, https://bible-history.com/old-testament/kings-prophets-nations.
108. "Bible Timeline," Bible Hub.
109. Multiple Faculty Contributors, "Introduction to Psalms," in *The Moody Bible Commentary,* ed. Michael Rydelnik and Michael VanLaningham (Chicago: Moody Publishers, 2014), 744.
110. Ibid.
111. "Psalms," in *New American Bible* (Collegeville, Minnesota: The Liturgical Press, 1991).
112. "Maskil," in *The Lexham Bible Dictionary*, ed. John D. Barry et al. (Bellingham, WA: Lexham Press, 2016).
113. "Lament," Merriam-Webster Dictionary, https://www.merriam-webster.com/dictionary/lament.

Made in United States
Orlando, FL
22 January 2024

42788453R00133